roasting
new healthy kitchen

RECIPES

Georgeanne Brennan

GENERAL EDITOR

Chuck Williams

PHOTOGRAPHY

Dan Goldberg

BONNIER BOOKS

contents

About this book

This volume of the New Healthy Kitchen was created to teach you how roasting can be a simple and appealing way to prepare nutrient-rich fruits, vegetables, legumes and grains as well as lean meats, poultry and seafood.

The foods you consume directly affect your overall health and energy level. Consequently, when you choose what to eat, you also choose how you will feel. Yet in today's modern world, the abundance of highly processed convenience foods often makes selecting healthy foods difficult. Thankfully, this doesn't have to be. This book will put you on the right track to adding fresh produce and whole grains to your diet—one of the best things you can to do live better.

The recipes in *Roasting* are organised in a new way: by the colour of the key vegetables or fruits used in the dish. This approach highlights the different nutritional benefits that each colour group contributes to your overall health. By thinking about the colours of foods, you can be sure to include all the fresh produce you need in your diet. If you consume at least one vegetable or fruit from each colour group daily, you can feel confident you are getting all the servings required for optimum health.

The New Healthy Kitchen series will help you prepare a wide variety of fresh fruits, vegetables and whole grains using especially healthy cooking techniques, helping you to bring colour and creativity to every meal you make.

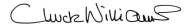

Eating the rainbow

Purple and blue fruits and vegetables contain fibre, vitamins and phytochemicals that promote heart health; help memory function; lower the risk of some cancers; promote urinary tract health and boost immunity

Green fruits and vegetables contain fibre, vitamins and phytochemicals that lower the risk of breast, prostate, lung and other cancers; promote eye health; help build strong bones and teeth and boost immunity

White and tan fruits and vegetables contain fibre, vitamins and phytochemicals that promote heart health; help maintain healthful cholesterol levels; lower the risk of breast, lung and other cancers and slow cholesterol absorption

Red fruits and vegetables contain fibre, vitamins and phytochemicals that promote heart health; help memory function; lower the risk of certain cancers; promote urinary tract health and boost immunity

Yellow and orange fruits and vegetables contain fibre, vitamins and phytochemicals that promote heart health; promote eye health; lower the risk of some cancers and boost immunity

Brown whole grains, legumes, seeds and nuts include fibre, vitamins, and phytonutrients that lower blood cholesterol levels and reduce the risk of colon and other cancers, diabetes, heart disease and stroke

Adapted from educational materials of the Produce for Better Health Foundation

The new healthy kitchen

Healthy meals demand high-quality fresh vegetables and fruits, grains and legumes, cooked without fuss to highlight their natural flavours and textures, and then presented beautifully to delight diners' eyes. Roasting is an excellent technique to use in the healthy kitchen because the dry heat brings out the inherent tastes of different foods but adds little excess fat and preserves valuable nutrients.

The philosophy of the New Healthy Kitchen series is simple and straightforward: the consumption of moderate amounts of a wide range of foods, especially peak-of-season produce and whole or minimally processed grains, is the key to a healthy diet. Instead of always counting calories, fat grams or carbohydrates, you need to focus on maintaining a constantly varied diet rich in fresh vegetables and fruits, whole grains

and legumes. If consuming such foods is the first priority of your daily regimen, a healthier balance of other foods will naturally follow.

People today, compared to earlier generations, consume a diet that is highly restricted in the kind of plant foods they eat. Our "feast or famine" instincts are at odds with the abundance of all types of food at our disposal, so we tend to overindulge in concentrated sources of energy, especially

animal fats. We also tend to gravitate toward carbohydrates, which are excellent sources of quick energy. However our most common forms of carbohydrates, such as refined flours, are also stripped of the wholesome nutrients found in whole grains.

While taking a daily multivitamin is not a bad idea, popping pills and supplements isn't the best solution to an ongoing lack of vitamins and minerals in your diet. Your body

can make better use of these compounds when it extracts them in their natural state from food. Eating a variety of plant foods is the best way of getting what you need, in a form in which your body is designed to get it.

Some of the benefits of eating fruits and vegetables come from the vitamins, minerals and fibre they contain, while the others come from a newly discovered class of nutrients called phytonutrients, or phytochemicals. These plant compounds work in a number of ways to protect our bodies and fight disease. In many cases, phytochemicals are the elements in plant foods that give them their distinctive colours and flavours. So the dazzling hues of vegetables and fruits, from bright red tomatoes to dark green spinach to deep

purple aubergine, give clues to the particular phytonutrients each contains. Eating a rainbow of produce will give you the broadest array of health benefits from all of these various nutrients.

But these colourful fruits and vegetables are not the only elements of a sound dietary regimen. Your daily intake must also include members of another important group of plant foods, grains and legumes, which are rich in fibre, protein, complex carbohydrates and minerals, as well as phytochemicals of their own. For the greatest nutritional benefit, the grains must be eaten whole or only minimally processed.

To guide your meal planning, the chapters in this cookbook are organised by the five prominent colour groups of vegetables and

fruits: purple and blue, green, white and tan, yellow and orange and red. A sixth chapter focuses on so-called brown foods, including whole grains, legumes, nuts and seeds. Concentrating on the colours of foods as you prepare meals will put a bounty of new, fresh ingredients onto your daily menu. Each colourful chapter begins with a chart showing which fruits and vegetables are at their peak of ripeness each season. The Brown chapter chart shows which grains or legumes might figure in a hearty main dish.

The recipes of the New Healthy Kitchen are typically quick and easy, designed for real-life cooks who don't have much time to spare, but who want to use the time they do have to cook and eat creatively, colourfully, and, most importantly, healthfully.

Fruits & vegetables

Fruits and vegetables are the cornerstone of a healthy diet. They are also some of the most beautiful and delicious foods on the planet—a boon to both the eye and the palate, with tastes and textures that range from bitter greens to sweet cherries. The recipes in *Roasting* will inspire you to add new fruits and vegetables to your meals and reap the benefits of their vitamins, minerals and phytochemicals.

In the early years of the twentieth century, scientists discovered, one after another, the various vitamins and minerals we now know are essential to maintaining good health and fighting disease. Today, we are entering into a similarly exciting era of discovery, as we learn about the roles that phytochemicals play in our bodies.

These protective compounds, which are believed to number in the thousands, work alone and in combination with one another and with nutrients. They work in different ways. For example, some phytochemicals act as antioxidants, protecting the body by neutralising unstable oxygen molecules (known as free radicals) that damage cells and promote disease. Regularly eating plant foods rich in antioxidants can reduce the risk of various cancers, heart disease, impaired vision and other illnesses.

Fruits and vegetables from each of the colour groups provide us with different combinations of phytonutrients, each playing a unique role in fighting disease and promoting health and well-being.

By eating fruit and vegetables at their peak of ripeness, you will not only be pleasing your palate, but you will also be giving your body the benefit of all the healthy nutrients that these foods contain.

Grains & legumes

Grains and legumes are traditional starchy accompaniments to meats and vegetables. The phrase *breaking bread* has long been synonymous with enjoying a meal, and legumes like chickpeas and kidney beans have sustained people in the Middle East and Latin America for generations. Don't let contemporary diet fads drive you away from these nourishing whole carbohydrates.

Grains and legumes, both of which are the seeds of plants, contain a wealth of nutrients. They are rich in vitamins and minerals and phytochemicals as well. Grains and legumes are also good sources of fibre, which keeps our digestive system in good working order and helps regulate the cholesterol levels in our blood.

Unfortunately, in our modern diet, grains are usually refined, in the form of white flour and white rice, with the fibre-rich hull and nutrient-rich germ removed. In addition, the amount of whole grains and legumes we consume overall has dropped sharply over the past few decades, most recently due to the popularity of low-carb diets.

In the New Healthy Kitchen, recipes that focus on grains, legumes, nuts and seeds are grouped in a chapter called Brown. These foods come in a variety of colours, but by thinking of them as brown it will help remind you that you should eat them in as close to their natural state as possible. Whole grains have more flavour than refined grains. Their superior taste, combined with high nutritional value, makes them equal companions to meats and vegetables on the dinner plate.

The recipes in this book encourage you to try a variety of grains, such as barley and millet, in their whole forms. It is worthwhile experimenting with other, less common types of whole grains, too, such as quinoa (pronounced KEEN-wah), an ancient grain native to the New World.

Legumes, which are the seeds of plants that split open when dried, include peas, beans, lentils and peanuts. They contain fibre, complex carbohydrates, phosphorus, and iron, plus plenty of protein: 50g (2oz) cooked dried beans or 1 tablespoon peanut butter equals 25g (1oz) of cooked meat, fish or poultry. And they are available in a wide range of appealing colours and shapes, from tiny brown lentils and smooth green lima beans to speckled cranberry beans.

Seeds and nuts (which are seeds, too) round out this earthy chapter and also play a role in a healthy diet.

All about roasting

Roasting or baking vegetables, fruits and grains on their own or in combination with meats, poultry or fish is a healthy way to cook. Dry-heat cooking forms a crust that helps to retain natural juices and nutrients, resulting in tasty and wholesome dishes. And unlike other techniques, such as frying or braising, very little fat is added or incorporated into the dish.

In this book, the terms *roasting* and *baking* are used to cover a variety of oven-cooked dishes. Although definitions vary, in general *roasting* is used to describe cooking a larger piece of food in an uncovered pan in the dry heat of the oven. *Baking* has a variety of different meanings, from cooking small pieces of savoury foods, sometimes covered, to cooking desserts in the oven. A handful of the dishes included here are cooked covered, but most are not. The recipes may be as simple as baked squash or roasted potatoes or as special as a raspberry gratin or a tomato tart. In general, little liquid is used in roasting or baking. Instead, the dry heat of the oven cooks the food. This is unlike braising or stewing, in which hot liquid and the vapours it produces cook the food.

In some cases, recipes begin with a cooker-top treatment, such as searing, boiling or steaming, and then the dish is slipped into the oven and roasted or baked. Searing is sometimes desirable for meat and poultry dishes. It browns them more fully than roasting alone, thereby enhancing both flavour and appearance. Other types of foods might need to be boiled or steamed to cook them partially before they are combined with other ingredients and baked. For example, spinach and dandelion greens are boiled and drained, and then used in a soufflé (page 42) and baked pasta dish (page 48), respectively, while lentils are cooked on the cooker top before they are mixed with seasonings for baked croquettes (page 113).

Conversely, foods might first be roasted or baked and then used as a component in a finished dish, such as Rib-eye Steaks with Baked Plums (page 105) or Baked Onion and White Aubergine Purée (page 59). Monkfish with Roasted White Corn Salsa (page 60) is another example, with the corn roasted and then used in a salsa.

In most cases, however, fruits or vegetables are roasted directly, such as in Roast Tuna with Olives, Grapes and Pine Nuts (page 24) or Roast Turkey Breast with Figs and Lavender (page 24).

Keep in mind these few tips for success. Make sure your ingredients, especially meat, poultry or fish, are patted dry before seasoning and cooking. This will prevent them from steaming and looking pale instead of roasting and browning. When oiling food for roasting, use only enough fat to keep the food from sticking to the pan or rack. Most of the ingredients used in these recipes have natural juices that keep them moist. Letting meat and poultry rest for several minutes after roasting will allow these juices to distribute evenly so the food is moist.

For the best results, always make sure your oven is set at the temperature indicated in the recipe. Cooking temperatures vary depending on what you are cooking and the desired texture of the finished dish. For example, to cook firm, dense winter squash all the way through requires long, slow cooking at a relatively low temperature, but raspberries and other tender fruits are best cooked quickly using high heat, so that they hold their shape and retain their flavour. Many ovens heat inaccurately. Use an oven thermometer to check yours and then adjust the dial if needed. Allow the oven to preheat for at least 20 minutes to ensure that it has reached the full temperature before roasting.

Whether you use a roasting pan or a baking dish, make sure it is solid and heavy, with shallow sides for good air circulation.

Creating the healthy meal

A commitment to eating a healthy diet based on vegetables, fruits, legumes and grains may require you to make some lifestyle changes. For example, you may need to modify your shopping habits, visiting the market more often for seasonal fresh produce, or to reduce the amount of meat you eat if you have grown accustomed to large portions. But the rewards will be quickly evident.

To find the best fresh produce, seek out just-harvested, locally grown vegetables and fruits in season at a good produce market or a natural-foods store. Or better yet, make a visit to the farmers' market one of your weekend outings. Although organic produce costs more, pesticide-free fruits and vegetables picked at the peak

of ripeness on local farms also taste better and are more densely packed with nutrients.

The colourful eating philosophy of the New Healthy Kitchen emphasises plant foods, but it doesn't exclude a variety of meats and dairy products. These ingredients add flavour, interest, texture and nutrients to a wide selection of healthy dishes.

Meat, dairy and other animal foods appeal to our bodies' craving for nutrient-rich calories, but it is easy to overindulge in these items, especially when you lead a typically sedentary modern life. The secret is to find balance in using and enjoying these ingredients. Animal foods contribute important proteins and vitamins to the diet, so they have a place in the New Healthy Kitchen. But they should play a co-starring role alongside vegetables and grains, rather than dominate the dinner plate. Keep your portions modest: a reasonable portion of cooked, boneless meat, poultry or seafood is about the size of a deck of playing cards. Remember, too, that certain meats and many cheeses can act as seasoning elements, rather than main events.

While too much fat adds excessive calories to the diet, a certain amount of fat is essential for the body to function properly. Fat also gives us the sensation of being satiated, which helps us to avoid overeating. Most of the recipes in this book use olive and rapeseed oils as the primary

fats for roasting. Along with grape seed oils, these oils have been proven beneficial, thanks in part to their monounsaturated fat content, which raises the level of HDL (good) cholesterol and lowers LDL (bad). Fish and shellfish contribute heart-healthy fats and play a key role in the New Healthy Kitchen.

Herbs and spices are essential flavour boosters in creating healthy dishes. A simple scattering of finely chopped fresh citrus zest or parsley adds not only colour and welcome flavour to so many different foods, but also valuable antioxidants. Vinegar and citrus juice are other important flavourings in the New Healthy Kitchen. They contribute an acidic note that heightens other flavours without making a dish taste heavy.

The simple decision to cook your meals at home, rather than order take-away or eat out, is an important step toward a healthier diet. The recipes in the New Healthy Kitchen are deliberately easy and streamlined. Preparation and cooking times are listed at the beginning of the recipe to help you fit them into your daily routine. Many dishes can be prepared in half an hour or a little more, making them perfect for a midweek supper. If you shop and cook more often, you will find that both activities become a habit, even if you a lead a busy life. And the rewards are great. Eating meals at home is often the highlight of the day. It bonds a family together and makes us appreciate all the wonderful foods nature has provided us.

aubergines prunes blackberries

PURPLE AND BLUE FRUITS AND VEGETABLES PROMOTE

purple radishes black currants

MEMORY FUNCTION • HELP PROMOTE URINARY TRACT

lavender blue potatoes purple

HEALTH • BOOST THE IMMUNE SYSTEM • HELP PROMOTE

cabbage raisins black grapes

HEALTHY AGEING • OFFER ANTIOXIDANTS FOR HEALING

purple figs blue plums purple

AND PROTECTION • HELP REDUCE THE RISK OF SOME

peppers black olives blueberries

CANCERS • PURPLE AND BLUE FRUITS AND VEGETABLES

Purple & blue

Purple and blue fruits and vegetables, once thought of as exotic in contrast with their green cousins, are becoming more and more common on dining tables. Their rising popularity is due in part to more people recognising their exceptional nutritional value. But it is also because their varied tastes, textures and appearances have caught the fancy of a growing fan club of home cooks.

Purple and blue fruits, such as fresh or dried blueberries, blackberries, figs, grapes and plums, are delicious eaten out of hand. But they can be roasted as well, and are versatile additions to every course of a meal, from starters to desserts.

Roasting black plums with just a small amount of star anise will heighten the sweetness of the fruit (page 34), while using grapes in a savoury dish with tuna balances the fruit's tartness (page 24).

Several of the blue and purple vegetables are more commonly known in other colours—think carrots, potatoes, peppers, asparagus and tomatoes—but the flavours, if not the colours, of these rich-hued vegetables are familiar ones. Blue potatoes, roasted until browned and crisp with rosemary, make a stunning alternative to common roasted potatoes, while purple carrots roasted with fennel and raisins bring colour to the table. Glossy purple aubergines turn into crunchy chips when thinly sliced and roasted (page 23).

SPRING	SUMMER	AUTUMN	WINTER
purple asparagus	purple peppers	purple-tipped Belgian endive	purple-tipped Belgian endive
purple-tipped Belgian endive	blackberries	purple peppers	purple cabbage
blueberries	blueberries	blueberries	purple carrots
purple cabbage	fresh blackcurrants	purple cabbage	currants
purple carrots	aubergine	purple carrots	blue, purple & black grapes
currants	purple figs	currants	black olives
blue, purple & black grapes	lavender	aubergine	blue potatoes
prunes	blue, purple & black plums	purple figs	prunes
raisins	purple & black tomatoes	blue, purple & black grapes	raisins
purple radish		blue, purple & black plums	
		blue potatoes	
		prunes	
		raisins	

aubergine crisps with yoghurt dipping sauce

2 very firm slender aubergines

2 Tbsp olive oil

250 g (8 oz) plain low-fat or whole yoghurt

1 cucumber, peeled and coarsely chopped

8 oil-packed sun-dried tomatoes, finely chopped

2 cloves garlic, finely chopped

Preheat oven to 200°C (400°F).

Using a mandoline or a sharp knife, cut aubergine into very thin rounds about 3 mm (⅛ in) thick. Arrange on a baking sheet in a single layer, using a second baking sheet if necessary. Drizzle with olive oil and turn to coat evenly.

Roast aubergine until golden on bottom, about 15 minutes. Turn slices and roast until golden brown on second side and crisp, about 15 minutes more.

Meanwhile, in a bowl, combine yoghurt, cucumber, sun-dried tomatoes, garlic and ¼ tsp salt and stir to mix well.

Remove aubergine crisps to paper towels to drain. Sprinkle with 2 tsp salt. Serve warm or at room temperature with yoghurt sauce.

To prepare: 10 minutes

To cook: 30 minutes

4 starter servings

roasted purple carrots & fennel

1 large or 2 medium fennel bulbs, trimmed (see Note)

250 g (8 oz) purple carrots, trimmed

1½ Tbsp olive oil

1 tsp fresh thyme leaves

1½ Tbsp Pernod

Preheat oven to 190°C (375°F).

Cut fennel bulb(s) in half from top to bottom, then cut each half into wedges about 12 mm (½ in) thick. Cut carrots in half crossways if quite long; otherwise, leave whole. Arrange carrots and fennel in a baking dish just large enough to hold them in a single layer. Drizzle with olive oil, sprinkle with thyme and ½ tsp salt and turn to coat evenly.

Roast until fennel has caramelised slightly and carrots have begun to wrinkle slightly, about 35 minutes. Remove from oven, pour Pernod over, and carefully light fumes with a long match. Shake pan slightly until flames go out. Serve at once.

Note: To trim fennel bulbs, cut off stems and feathery tops and any bruised outer stalks.

To prepare: 5 minutes

To cook: 35 minutes

4 side-dish servings

roasted tuna with olives, grapes & pine nuts

3 Tbsp olive oil

185 g (6 oz) seedless purple grapes, some cut in half

75 g (2½ oz) stoned oil-cured black olives, coarsely chopped

4 tuna steaks, each about 155 g (5 oz) and 12 mm (½ in) thick

3 Tbsp pine nuts

Preheat oven to 230°C (450°F).

Pour 1 Tbsp olive oil into a shallow baking dish just large enough to hold tuna steaks in a single layer. Add grapes and olives and turn to coat evenly with oil. Arrange tuna steaks among olives and grapes, season with 1 tsp salt and 1 tsp pepper, and drizzle with 2 Tbsp olive oil. Sprinkle pine nuts over all. Roast until lower one-third of tuna steaks are opaque, about 10 minutes. Turn tuna steaks and cook until second side is opaque but tuna is still pink in centre for medium-rare, 5–8 minutes more.

To serve, place a tuna steak on each warmed plate and spoon grape and olive mixture alongside.

To prepare: 5 minutes

To cook: 15 minutes

4 servings

roasted turkey breast with figs & lavender

1 turkey breast, 1.25 kg (2½ lb)

1 tsp dried lavender blossoms, crushed

125 g (4 oz) dried purple figs, coarsely chopped

2 Tbsp finely chopped shallot

125 ml (4 fl oz) low-salt chicken stock

1 Tbsp balsamic vinegar

Preheat oven to 190°C (375°F). Rub turkey breast all over with lavender blossoms, 1 tsp salt and 1 tsp pepper. Place in a shallow, flameproof roasting pan and roast, basting occasionally with pan juices, until skin is golden brown and juices run clear when pierced to bone with a sharp knife, about 40 minutes.

Remove from oven and remove turkey from pan. Make a bed of figs and shallot in roasting pan, then put turkey on top and add 3 Tbsp of chicken stock to the pan. Return pan to oven and roast until figs are soft and shallot is translucent, 10–15 minutes.

Remove turkey breast to a carving board, tent loosely with foil, and rest for 10 minutes. Place roasting pan on a burner or two over medium-high heat. Add remaining 5 Tbsp chicken stock and vinegar and cook, stirring to scrape up browned bits from bottom of pan and mashing figs to make a thick sauce, about 1 minute.

Carve turkey into slices 12 mm (½ in) thick, arrange overlapping on a warmed platter, and drizzle with pan sauce. Serve at once.

To prepare: 10 minutes

To cook: 1 hour, plus 10 minutes to rest

6 servings

roasted chicken with purple cabbage

½ head purple cabbage, cored and coarsely chopped

1 roasting chicken, 1.5–1.75 kg (3–3½ lb)

1 Tbsp plus 2 tsp olive oil

1 Tbsp butter

2 slices bacon, coarsely chopped

45 g (1½ oz) finely chopped onion

½ tsp caraway seeds

250 ml (8 fl oz) low-salt chicken stock

4 tablespoons balsamic vinegar

To prepare: 10 minutes

To cook: 1¼–1½ hours, plus 10 minutes to rest

4 servings

Preheat oven to 180°C (350°F). Position racks in oven for roasting a chicken and a baking dish of cabbage at the same time. Put cabbage in a bowl with cold water to cover and set aside.

Rub outside of chicken with 2 tsp olive oil and season inside and out with 1 tsp salt and ½ tsp pepper. Place in a shallow, flameproof roasting pan just large enough to fit it without crowding and roast, basting the bird with pan juices after 30 minutes and then occasionally thereafter, until skin is golden brown and juices run clear when a thigh joint is pierced with a sharp knife, 1¼–1½ hours, depending on size of chicken.

While chicken is roasting, prepare cabbage. In a small lidded frying pan over medium heat, melt butter with 1 Tbsp olive oil. Add bacon and sauté until it begins to sizzle, about 2 minutes. Reduce heat to low and cook slowly, stirring occasionally, until bacon fat is rendered, about 5 minutes longer. Remove from heat. Using a slotted spoon, remove bacon and reserve for another use. Return pot to medium heat. Sauté onion and caraway seeds until onion is soft, 3–4 minutes. Drain cabbage well, add to pot and cook, stirring, until it glistens, 2–3 minutes. Stir in the chicken stock, transfer to a baking dish, cover, and place in oven. Bake, stirring occasionally, until cabbage is tender and some stock has been absorbed, about 1 hour. Drain cabbage in a colander set over a bowl, reserving 2 Tbsp cooking liquid.

When chicken is done, remove to a board, reserving pan juices. Tent loosely with foil and rest for 10 minutes. Discard all but 2 Tbsp of juices from roasting pan. Place pan on cooker top over medium-high heat. Add vinegar and reserved cabbage liquid and stir to scrape up browned bits from bottom of pan. Add cabbage, turn to coat, and cook until heated through, about 2 minutes. Season with salt and pepper.

Carve chicken into serving pieces. Make a bed of cabbage on a warmed platter and arrange chicken on top. Serve at once.

roasted aubergine, asian style

Cut slender aubergines in half lengthways, drizzle with oil, sprinkle with finely chopped garlic and roast in a hot oven until tender. Drizzle with soy sauce and sprinkle with toasted sesame seeds and chopped basil before serving.

baked stuffed blue potatoes

Bake potatoes until tender. Cut in half lengthways, scoop out flesh and mix with butter, grated Gruyère cheese and salt and pepper. Refill potato shells, then top with a little more grated cheese and put under grill until tops are golden.

sweet blueberry flat bread

Roll out your favourite pizza dough into a round. Transfer to a baking sheet. Sprinkle with sugar and cover with blueberries. Sprinkle with more sugar and dot with butter. Bake like a pizza until crust browns and berries bubble.

raisin & prune chutney with lemon

In a baking dish, combine raisins, chopped prunes and onion, brown sugar, lemon juice and zest, balsamic vinegar and a small amount of water. Cover and bake at 150°C (300°F), stirring occasionally, until juices thicken, about 40 minutes.

roasted pork & prunes

1 boneless pork loin roast, 750 g–1 kg (1½–2 lb)

1 Tbsp olive oil

1 tsp paprika

1 tsp dried sage, crushed

4 slices bacon, coarsely chopped

2 Tbsp finely chopped shallot

4 tablespoons dry white wine

280 g (9 oz) stoned prunes

Preheat oven to 200°C (400°F). Rub pork all over with ½ Tbsp olive oil, then rub with paprika, sage 1 tsp salt and 1 tsp pepper.

Heat ½ Tbsp olive oil in a frying pan over medium-high heat. Add bacon and sauté until it is sizzling, about 2 minutes. Reduce heat to low and continue cooking, stirring occasionally, until fat is rendered and bacon is crisp, about 5 minutes more. Remove from heat. Using a slotted spoon, remove bacon to paper towels to drain, leaving fat in pan.

Return pan to medium-high heat. When fat is hot, add pork and sear until bottom is browned, about 3 minutes. Using tongs to turn and hold pork, brown all other sides, 2–3 minutes per side. Add shallot while browning last side, stirring to coat. Remove pork to a platter. Raise heat to high, add 2 Tbsp wine, and stir to scrape up browned bits from bottom of pan. Return bacon to pan and stir to combine, then pour contents of pan into a shallow, flameproof roasting pan. Add pork and any accumulated juices from platter.

Roast for 15 minutes. Remove from oven, surround roast with prunes, add remaining 2 Tbsp wine to pan and return to oven. Reduce heat to 190°C (375°F) and continue roasting until pork registers 60°–63°C (140°–145°F) on a meat thermometer, about 30 minutes more.

Remove roast to a carving board, tent loosely with foil, and rest for 10 minutes. Carve roast into slices 2.5 cm (1 in) thick. Arrange slices overlapping on a warmed platter. Place roasting pan on cooker top over medium heat and gently reheat prunes and pan juices. Spoon prunes and juices down centre or alongside sliced roast. Serve at once.

To prepare: 10 minutes

To cook: 1 hour, plus 10 minutes to rest

4–6 servings

baked pilaf with currants, lavender & almonds

105 g (3½ oz) long-grain white rice

90 g (3 oz) wild rice

1 Tbsp butter

1 stick celery, finely chopped

2 Tbsp finely chopped onion

60 g (2 oz) currants

75 g (2½ oz) chopped almonds, toasted (see Note, page 70)

80 ml (3 fl oz) orange juice

1 tsp dried lavender blossoms, crushed

1 orange, peeled and cut crossways into slices 6 mm (¼ in) thick

In a saucepan over medium-high heat, bring 250 ml (8 fl oz) water to the boil and stir in ½ tsp salt. Add white rice, return to the boil, cover, and reduce heat to low. Cook until rice is tender and water is absorbed, about 20 minutes. Remove from heat and set aside.

Meanwhile, in another saucepan over medium-high heat, bring 375 ml (12 fl oz) water to the boil, stir in ½ tsp salt and add wild rice. Return to the boil, cover and reduce heat to low. Cook until rice grains have plumped and most of water is absorbed, about 45 minutes. Drain rice well in a colander.

Preheat oven to 190°C (375°F) and lightly butter a medium baking dish. In a frying pan over medium-high heat, melt butter. When it foams, add celery, onion, currants and half the almonds. Reduce heat to medium and sauté until celery and onion are translucent, about 2 minutes. Add white rice and wild rice and cook, stirring, until rice glistens, 2–3 minutes more. Add orange juice, lavender, 1 tsp salt and ½ tsp pepper. Taste and adjust seasoning.

Spoon pilaf into prepared baking dish. Spread evenly, then sprinkle with remaining almonds. Arrange orange slices on top. Bake until pilaf is heated throughout and orange slices have softened slightly, about 30 minutes. Serve hot, directly from baking dish.

To prepare: 10 minutes

To cook: 1 hour 20 minutes

4 side-dish servings

roasted blue potatoes with herb tattoos

2 Tbsp olive oil

8 medium or 16 small blue potatoes, scrubbed and halved lengthways

Leaves from 4–6 sprigs rosemary

Preheat oven to 190°C (375°F).

Drizzle olive oil into a baking dish. Add potatoes and turn to coat on all sides. Remove to a baking sheet and arrange cut side up. Gently press 8–10 rosemary leaves onto surface of each in an attractive pattern. Sprinkle with 1 tsp salt.

Roast until potatoes are easily pierced through to their centres with the tip of a sharp knife, about 1 hour. Serve hot.

To prepare: 10 minutes

To cook: 1 hour

4 side-dish servings

purple fruits with lavender syrup

125g (4 oz) plus 2 Tbsp sugar

6 fresh, pesticide-free lavender sprigs
or 1 teaspoon dried lavender flowers,
plus more for garnish

1½ tsp butter

4 purple plums, halved and stoned

20 black grapes

The day before serving, in a small saucepan, combine 250 ml (8 fl oz) water and **125g (4 oz)** sugar and bring to the boil over high heat. Reduce heat to medium and stir until sugar is dissolved, 10 minutes. Add lavender, cover and stand overnight. The following day, strain syrup through a fine-mesh sieve lined with several layers of damp cheesecloth. Return to a clean saucepan, bring to the boil and cook until reduced by one-half, about 5 minutes. Remove from heat and let cool.

Preheat oven to 200°C (400°F).

Butter a baking dish just large enough to hold fruit in a single layer. Add plums, cut side down and grapes. Sprinkle with 2 Tbsp sugar and dot with butter. Bake until butter and sugar have melted and the skin of the plums and grapes is just beginning to wrinkle, 8–10 minutes.

Remove and leave to stand for 10 minutes. Gently spoon fruit into dessert bowls or glasses and drizzle with lavender syrup. Garnish each with lavender and serve warm.

To prepare: 24 hours for syrup

To cook: 10 minutes

4 servings

roasted black plums with star anise

2 tsp butter

4 black plums, halved and stoned

4 tsp palm sugar (see Notes)

8 star anise pods (see Notes)

Preheat oven to 190°C (375°F). Lightly butter a baking dish just large enough to hold plum halves in a single layer. Arrange plums, cut side up, in prepared dish.

Place ½ tsp sugar in cavity of each plum half, then place a star anise pod on top. Roast until sugar has melted, plums are heated through, and skins are just beginning to wrinkle a bit on the edges, about 15 minutes.

Serve hot or warm.

Notes: Palm sugar, also called jaggery, can be found in Asian and Indian markets. Star anise is inedible but makes for a pretty presentation; instruct diners to remove before eating. Or remove before serving. Serve with vanilla ice cream, if desired.

To prepare: 5 minutes

To cook: 15 minutes

4 dessert servings

sprouting broccoli cucumbers

GREEN FRUITS AND VEGETABLES BOOST THE IMMUNE

spinach kale watercress avocados

SYSTEM • PROMOTE EYE HEALTH • HELP BUILD STRONG

asparagus broccoli snow peas

BONES • BUILD STRONG TEETH • OFFER ANTIOXIDANTS

leeks lettuce courgette green

FOR HEALING AND PROTECTION • REDUCE THE RISK OF

grapes endive brussels sprouts

CERTAIN CANCERS • GREEN FRUITS AND VEGETABLES

limes rocket kiwifruits artichokes

BOOST THE IMMUNE SYSTEM • PROMOTE EYE HEALTH

Green

Although we mostly associate the colour green with crisp, leafy vegetables such as lettuce, chard, spinach and sprouting broccoli, even referring to them as greens, green embraces a vast range of fruits and vegetables, each of them distinct. Delicate spinach and lettuce are very different from robust artichokes or celery, and bear no resemblance to solid heads of Brussels sprouts or broccoli.

Crunchy green apples and pears, summer's soft green grapes, silky-smooth avocados, crisp cucumbers and asparagus, peas, and peppers—all exemplify the diversity of green fruits and vegetables. A wide range of fruits and vegetables from the green family take well to roasting in a hot oven. Green apples, with their sturdy flesh, are perfect to stuff and bake (page 52); cucumbers create a delicate roasting bed for cod with Thai seasonings (page 45); and sprouting broccoli roasted with lemon makes a simple but flavorful side dish (page 41). Tomatillos, which look like small green tomatoes, (but are not related), and are one of the lesser known green vegetables, are cooked with chicken and chiles to create a spicy main dish with a Southwestern accent (page 51).

As this chapter will illustrate, even leafy greens, such as spinach, chard, and dandelion greens, can be cooked in the oven, contributing their flavors to a soufflé (page 42), a baked pasta (page 48), and a cheese-topped gratin.

SPRING	SUMMER	AUTUMN	WINTER
artichokes	rocket	green apples	green apples
asparagus	avocados (Hass)	artichokes	bok choy
green peppers	green chillis	bok choy	broccoli
endive	cucumbers	broccoli	broccoli rabe
fava beans	dandelion greens	broccoli rabe	sprouting broccoli
green beans	green beans	brussels sprouts	brussels sprouts
limes	green figs	green cabbage	green cabbage
lettuce	herbs	endive	celery
green pears	limes	green grapes	endive
peas	green-fleshed melons	kale	kale
snow peas	okra	leeks	leeks
sugar snap peas	spinach	green pears	snow peas
spinach	tomatillos	Swiss chard	spinach
watercress	courgettes	watercress	watercress

roasted sprouting broccoli with lemon

1½ Tbsp olive oil

2 cloves garlic, finely chopped

1 bunch sprouting broccoli, trimmed and coarsely chopped

½ lemon, not peeled, seeded and cut into 6-mm (¼-in) dice

Preheat oven to 180°C (350°F). Heat 1 Tbsp olive oil in a frying pan over medium-high heat. Add garlic and sauté until lightly golden, about 1 minute, then add sprouting broccoli, lemon and ½ tsp salt. Sauté just until colour of sprouting broccoli deepens, about 1 minute more.

Remove contents of frying pan to a medium oven proof baking dish, add ½ Tbsp olive oil and turn to coat. Roast until sprouting broccoli is tender-crisp, 10–12 minutes. Remove to a bowl or platter and serve hot or cooled to room temperature.

To prepare: 5 minutes

To cook: 15 minutes

3 or 4 side-dish servings

roasted courgettes with anchoïade

2 courgettes

1 Tbsp olive oil

1 tsp fresh thyme leaves

Anchïoade
80–125 ml (3–4 fl oz) extra-virgin olive oil

1 tin (75 g / 2½ oz) anchovy fillets, rinsed and drained

3 cloves garlic, finely chopped

Preheat oven to 400°F (200°C).

Cut courgettes in half crossways. Cut each half lengthways into 3 even slices. Arrange slices in a baking dish just large enough to hold them in a single layer. Drizzle with olive oil and sprinkle with thyme. Season with ½ tsp salt and ½ tsp pepper and turn to coat evenly.

Roast until bottoms are golden brown, 15–20 minutes. Turn and roast until golden on second side and tender-crisp, 5–10 minutes more.

For Anchïoade: In a small frying pan over low heat, heat 80ml (3 fl oz) olive oil. Add anchovies and garlic and cook, mashing anchovies until they dissolve into oil to make a paste, about 3 minutes. Gradually stir in enough of remaining oil to give sauce consistency of a thick vinaigrette.

Serve courgettes warm, accompanied with *anchoïade*.

To prepare: 10 minutes

To cook: 30 minutes

3 or 4 starter servings

spinach soufflé

1 Tbsp grated Parmesan cheese

185 g (6 oz) packed spinach leaves (about 1 bunch)

4½ Tbsp (70 g / 2¼ oz) butter

2 Tbsp finely chopped shallot

45 g (1½ oz) plain flour

⅛ tsp freshly grated nutmeg

250 ml (8 fl oz) semi-skimmed or whole milk

4 whole eggs, separated, plus 2 egg whites, at room temperature

To prepare: 20 minutes
To cook: 55 minutes
4 servings

Preheat oven to 190°C (375°F). Butter bottom and sides of a 1 litre (1¾ pt) soufflé dish. Sprinkle bottom with Parmesan, then turn dish on its side, tapping and turning to coat all sides with cheese. Set aside.

In a large saucepan over high heat, bring 1 litre (32 fl oz) water to the boil. Add spinach, reduce heat to medium and cook until spinach is wilted but still bright green, about 4 minutes. Remove to a colander and rinse under cold running water until cool. Drain thoroughly, squeeze out excess water and chop coarsely. In a frying pan over medium-high heat, melt 1 Tbsp butter. When it foams, add shallot and cook, stirring, until translucent, about 1 minute. Add spinach and cook, stirring, until it glistens, about 2 minutes. Set aside.

In a medium saucepan over medium-high heat, melt 3½ Tbsp butter. When it foams, remove from heat and whisk in flour, nutmeg, 1 tsp salt, and ¼ tsp pepper. Return to medium-high heat and add milk slowly, whisking constantly. Cook, whisking occasionally, until taste of flour is gone and sauce is thickened and smooth, about 5 minutes. Remove from heat and leave to cool for 2–3 minutes.

In a bowl, using an electric mixer or a whisk, beat 6 egg whites until stiff peaks form when beater or whisk is lifted. In another bowl, beat 4 egg yolks until creamy.

Whisk egg yolks into cooled white sauce until well blended. Stir in spinach mixture. Stir about 3 Tbsp egg whites into spinach mixture to lighten it, then use a spatula to gently fold in remaining egg whites just until no white streaks remain. Scrape into prepared soufflé dish.

Bake until top has puffed and is golden brown, about 40 minutes. Serve hot, directly from dish.

roasted asparagus
with eggs & parmesan

500 g (1 lb) asparagus, trimmed

1 Tbsp olive oil

1 tsp vinegar

4 eggs

1 Tbsp grated Parmesan cheese

Preheat oven to 230°C (450°F). Arrange asparagus in a single layer in a baking dish. Drizzle with olive oil, sprinkle with ¼ tsp salt and ¼ tsp pepper, and turn to coat evenly. Roast, turning occasionally, until tips are lightly browned and asparagus is tender-crisp, 15–20 minutes. Remove to a platter and tent loosely with foil.

Fill a deep sauté pan with cold water. Add vinegar and a pinch of salt and set pan over medium heat. When water begins to simmer, break eggs, one at a time, into a cup and slip each gently into the water. Keeping water at a low simmer, poach to desired doneness, 3–5 minutes. Using a slotted spoon, remove eggs and blot dry.

To serve, divide asparagus spears among plates and top each portion with a poached egg and a sprinkle of Parmesan, salt, and pepper.

To prepare: 10 minutes

To cook: 25 minutes

4 starter servings

cod on a bed
of cucumbers

1½ cucumbers, peeled, halved lengthways, and seeded

2 tsp Asian fish sauce

½ tsp palm or raw sugar (see Notes, page 34)

2 Tbsp lime juice

2.5-cm (1-in) piece lemongrass, bruised (see Note)

4 cod fillets, each about 155 g (5 oz) and 12 mm (½ in) thick

1 Tbsp finely chopped fresh chives

2 Tbsp chopped fresh basil

Preheat oven to 230°C (450°F).

Cut cucumber halves on diagonal into long slices about 6 mm (¼ in) thick. Arrange slices overlapping in bottom of a baking dish just large enough to hold cod fillets in a single layer.

In a small bowl, stir together fish sauce, sugar and lime juice. Tuck lemongrass into cucumber slices and arrange fillets in a single layer on top of cucumbers. Drizzle with fish sauce mixture. Cover dish tightly with foil and bake until fish is opaque throughout and flakes easily with a fork, 12–15 minutes.

Garnish with chives and basil and serve directly from baking dish, slipping a spatula beneath cucumbers.

Note: To prepare lemongrass, cut off and discard top of stalk, then remove tough outer layer from bulbous lower portion. Crush lightly with flat side of a chef's knife to bruise, which releases flavoursome oils.

To prepare: 10 minutes

To cook: 15 minutes

4 servings

chillis stuffed with goat's cheese

Slit large chillis and remove seeds and membranes. Stuff with mashed mixture of goat's cheese, milk, chives, shallot and salt. Roast at 200°C (400°F) in a lightly oiled baking dish until soft and slightly wrinkled, 30–40 minutes.

sautéed spinach with peanuts & soy sauce

Sauté finely chopped shallot or onion in peanut oil until softened. Toss with spinach and chopped peanuts, drizzle with just enough soy sauce to season and bake at 180°C (350°F) until spinach is dark and wilted, 11–15 minutes.

broccoli baked with garlic & chilli

Chop broccoli and put in a baking dish. Add olive oil to come 6 mm (¼ in) up sides of dish. Season with finely chopped garlic, red pepper flakes, salt and pepper. Turn to coat evenly. Cover and bake in a 120°C (250°F) oven until tender.

gratinéed swiss chard

Stem chard and cook in salted boiling water until tender. Chop, drain and place in a baking dish. Sprinkle with olive oil, salt and pepper and turn to coat. Top with grated Parmesan, dot with butter and bake in a hot oven until golden.

baked pasta with dandelion greens & sausage

250 g (8 oz) orecchiette pasta

2 Tbsp olive oil

3 chicken-fennel or other mild sausages

1 bunch dandelion greens, about 375 g (12 oz), tough stems removed, leaves coarsely chopped

250 g (8 oz) whole-milk ricotta cheese

1 Tbsp butter

15 g (½ oz) fresh breadcrumbs (see Notes, page 117)

Bring a large pot of salted water to the boil over high heat. Add orecchiette and reduce heat to medium. Stir once or twice and cook until al dente, about 15 minutes. Drain thoroughly and place in a medium baking dish. Drizzle with 1 Tbsp olive oil, sprinkle with 1 tsp salt and 1 tsp pepper and stir to mix well.

Preheat oven to 180°C (350°F).

In a frying pan, heat 1 Tbsp olive oil over medium-high heat. When oil is hot, add sausages and sauté, turning as needed, until browned on all sides, about 10 minutes. Remove to a cutting board and leave to cool slightly. Meanwhile, add dandelion greens to pan and sauté over medium-high heat until tender but still bright green, 5 minutes. Remove from heat.

Cut sausages into 2.5-cm (1-in) slices and add to pasta with greens and pan juices. Toss and stir until ingredients are evenly distributed. Taste and adjust seasoning. Spoon ricotta onto pasta and spread it evenly over the top.

In a small frying pan over medium heat, melt butter. When it foams, add breadcrumbs and cook, stirring often, until golden, 3–4 minutes. Sprinkle toasted crumbs evenly over ricotta.

Bake until cheese is lightly browned around edges, 25–30 minutes. Serve hot, directly from baking dish.

To prepare: 10 minutes

To cook: 1 hour

4 servings

duck & brussels sprouts

1 whole duck leg with thigh, about 250 g (8 oz)

1 Tbsp olive oil

3–4 Tbsp hazelnut oil

500 g (1 lb) Brussels sprouts, trimmed and quartered

80 ml (3 fl oz) dry vermouth or white wine

60 g (2 oz) skinned toasted hazelnuts (see Note, page 70), chopped

Preheat oven to 180°C (350°F). Rub duck leg with olive oil, ½ tsp salt and ½ tsp pepper. Place duck in a shallow roasting dish just large enough to fit it and roast until skin is golden brown and flesh is tender, about 1¼ hours. Remove from oven but leave oven on.

In an ovenproof sauté pan, heat 1 Tbsp hazelnut oil over medium-high heat. Add Brussels sprouts and sauté just until beginning to turn golden, about 3 minutes. Add duck and any pan juices and turn to coat. Raise heat to high and add vermouth, stirring to scrape up any browned bits from bottom of pan.

Cover pan and place in oven. Bake until duck shreds easily and Brussels sprouts are tender, about 20 minutes. Remove from heat and remove duck to a cutting board. When duck is cool enough to handle, pull meat from bones and shred or chop coarsely. Discard skin and bones, add meat to pan with Brussels sprouts and toss to combine. Add toasted hazelnuts and drizzle with 2–3 Tbsp hazelnut oil. Season with salt and pepper to taste. Serve warm or at room temperature.

To prepare: 25 minutes

To cook: 1 hour 35 minutes

3 or 4 servings

tomatillo casserole

750 g (1½ lb) skinless, boneless chicken breasts, cut into cubes

½ tsp ground cumin

2 Tbsp rapeseed or grape seed oil, plus more as needed

60 g (2 oz) finely chopped onion

500 g (1 lb) tomatillos, husked, rinsed and quartered

3 chillis, seeded and finely chopped

4 cloves garlic, finely chopped

1 tsp dried oregano

2 Tbsp dry white wine

250 ml (8 fl oz) low-salt chicken stock

1 tin (15 oz/470 g) hominy, rinsed and drained

Preheat oven to 180°C (350°F). Put chicken in a bowl. Add cumin, 1 tsp salt and 1 tsp pepper and turn to coat evenly.

In an ovenproof sauté pan, heat 1 Tbsp oil over medium-high heat. When oil is hot, add half of the chicken. Cook, turning as needed, until chicken is nearly opaque throughout, about 3 minutes. Remove to a platter and cook remaining chicken in same way, adding a little more oil if needed. Remove second batch to platter. Add 1 Tbsp oil to pan and sauté onion until translucent, about 3 minutes. Add tomatillos, chillis, garlic, chicken and juices from platter, oregano, white wine and chicken stock and stir to combine. Taste and adjust seasoning.

Cover pan and place in oven. Bake, stirring occasionally, until the tomatillos have broken down to make a thick sauce, 30 minutes. Add hominy, re-cover, and cook until hominy is heated through, 10–15 minutes more. Ladle into warmed bowls and serve hot.

To prepare: 20 minutes

To cook: 50 minutes

4 servings

green apples baked with dried cranberries

4 large green-skinned apples such as Granny Smith

105 g (3½ oz) firmly packed light brown sugar

60 g (2 oz) dried cranberries

2 Tbsp butter

Double cream for serving (optional)

Preheat oven to 180°C (350°F).

Using an apple corer, cut cores from apples in neat plugs. In a small bowl, combine sugar and cranberries. Divide mixture evenly among apples, stuffing into cavities. Place apples in a deep baking dish just large enough to hold them. Pour in enough water to cover the bottom of the pan by 6 mm (¼ in). Put pan in oven and bake until apples have turned golden brown, are slightly shrunken, and are easily pierced with a fork, about 1 hour.

Place apples onto dessert plates and drizzle each with cream, if desired. Serve hot or warm.

To prepare: 15 minutes

To cook: 1 hour

Serves 4

green pear & grape clafoutis

1 firm but ripe green pear such as Williams'

2 eggs

125 ml (4 fl oz) double cream

250 ml (8 fl oz) semi-skimmed or whole milk

125 g (4 oz) sugar

105 g (3½ oz) plain flour

1 tsp butter

90 g (3 oz) seedless green grapes

Preheat oven to 180°C (350°F). Halve and core pear and cut into 6-mm (¼-in) dice. Set aside. Butter a baking dish just large enough to hold diced pear in a single layer.

In a bowl, using an electric mixer or a whisk, beat together eggs, cream, milk and 75 g (2½ oz) sugar until well combined. Sprinkle in flour and beat until flour is incorporated and batter is smooth.

Cover bottom of prepared baking dish with diced pear, patting into a single layer. Layer grapes on top. Sprinkle with 3 Tbsp sugar. Pour batter over. Bake until golden and puffed, about 45 minutes. Serve clafoutis hot or warm.

To prepare: 10 minutes

To cook: 45 minutes

4–6 dessert servings

cauliflower shallots mushrooms

WHITE AND TAN FRUITS AND VEGETABLES CONTAIN

dates jicama bananas tan figs

ANTIOXIDANTS FOR HEALING AND PROTECTION • HELP

fennel bulbs turnips white corn

MAINTAIN A HEALTHY CHOLESTEROL LEVEL • PROMOTE

potatoes jerusalem artichokes

HEART HEALTH • BOOST THE IMMUNE SYSTEM • SLOW

ginger kohlrabi white aubergines

CHOLESTEROL ABSORPTION • WHITE AND TAN FRUITS

parsnips white nectarines garlic

AND VEGETABLES OFFER ANTIOXIDANTS FOR HEALING

White & tan

At first glance, the muted, neutral hues of white and tan fruits and vegetables might make you think they are bland, but in fact many of them boast excellent flavour. Among them are members of the Allium genus—garlic, onions, shallots, leeks—that are invaluable for providing an aromatic base in countless dishes and for their wealth of phytochemicals.

Potatoes, one of the strongest workhorses of the kitchen, belong here. So do the sturdy root vegetables—turnips, celeriac and parsnips—all of which are ideal for roasting, as the dry heat of the oven brings out their natural sweetness.

Here, too, you'll find mushrooms, such as the meaty field mushroom, which when roasted with garlic and parsley makes a meatless meal on its own (page 69). The most elegant member of the brassica family is white: cauliflower. Just like potatoes, the crunch of celery root, is perfect for a gratin (page 66). The crunchy Jerusalem artichoke, is also refered to as a sunchoke, displays its irresistible nutty flavour to perfection when it is roasted with cream and then drizzled with delicate white truffle oil (page 59).

The tan and white fruits, while not in abundance, include pears, figs and the potassium-rich banana, as well as white nectarines and peaches in their brief season. All can be baked and paired with meats or served alone as a finishing touch to a meal.

SPRING	SUMMER	AUTUMN	WINTER
white asparagus	bananas	bananas	cauliflower
bananas	white corn	cauliflower	celeriac
cauliflower	white aubergine	dates	dates
dates	tan figs	tan figs	garlic
garlic	garlic	Jerusalem artichokes	ginger
ginger	kohlrabi	jicama	Jerusalem artichokes
jicama	mushrooms	kohlrabi	jicama
mushrooms	white nectarines	mushrooms	dried mushrooms
onions	onions	onions	onions
parsnips	white peaches	parsnips	parsnips
tan pears	tan pears	tan pears	tan pears
potatoes	plantains	potatoes	potatoes
shallots	potatoes	shallots	shallots
turnips	shallots	turnips	turnips

baked onion & white aubergine purée

1 large white round aubergine, quartered

1 tsp olive oil

2 onions, quartered

4 cloves garlic, peeled but left whole

2 tsp finely chopped fresh thyme

1 tsp lemon juice

Flat bread or crackers for serving

Preheat oven to 180°C (350°F). Lightly oil a small baking dish.

Rub aubergine quarters with olive oil. Arrange aubergine, onions and garlic in prepared dish and cover tightly with foil. Roast until vegetables are very tender, about 1 hour. Let cool.

When aubergine is cool enough to handle, scoop flesh from skin into blender or food processor with a large spoon. (Discard skin.) Add other roasted vegetables, thyme, lemon juice, 1 tsp salt and ½ tsp pepper and process until smooth. Taste and adjust seasoning. Serve with flat bread or crackers.

To prepare: 10 minutes, plus 20 minutes to cool

To cook: 1 hour

4 starter servings

mashed jerusalem artichokes with truffle oil

750 g (1½ lb) Jerusalem artichokes

1½ tsp olive oil

2 Tbsp double cream

1 tsp white or black truffle oil (see Note)

Preheat oven to 180°C (350°F). Place Jerusalem artichokes in a baking dish and rub with olive oil. Roast until fork-tender, about 45 minutes. Remove from oven and set aside until cool enough to handle.

Peel Jerusalem artichokes with a paring knife or vegetable peeler and place in a bowl. Add cream, 1 tsp salt and ½ tsp pepper and mash with a fork or potato masher to a smooth paste. Taste and adjust seasoning with salt and pepper. Scoop into a serving dish and drizzle with truffle oil. Serve at once, directly from dish.

Note: Use white truffle oil for a subtle earthy flavour, or black truffle oil for more pronounced taste.

To prepare: 5 minutes

To cook: 45 minutes

4 side-dish servings

monkfish with roasted white corn salsa

2 ears white corn, husks and silk removed

3½ tsp corn oil

1 tsp mild paprika

1 avocado, stoned, peeled and cut into small dice

4 tomatillos, husked, rinsed and finely chopped

2 Tbsp finely chopped coriander

2 serrano chillis, seeded and finely chopped

3 Tbsp lime juice

30 g (1 oz) crumbled feta cheese

655 g (1⅓ lb) monkfish, membrane removed, cut into slices 2.5 cm (1 in) thick

Preheat oven to 200°C (400°F). Rub corn with 2 tsp oil and season with paprika and salt and pepper to taste. Place in a baking dish and roast, turning occasionally, until kernels are lightly browned and beginning to wrinkle, 35–40 minutes. Remove from oven and set aside to cool. Raise oven temperature to 230°C (450°F). Lightly oil another baking dish just large enough to accommodate the fish medallions in a single layer.

When corn is cool enough to handle, use a heavy, sharp knife to cut kernels from cobs into a bowl. Add avocado, tomatillos, coriander, chillis and lime juice. Toss gently until ingredients are evenly distributed. Sprinkle with cheese. Set aside.

Season fish with salt and pepper and arrange in a single layer in prepared baking dish. Drizzle with 1½ tsp oil and turn to coat evenly. Roast until fish is opaque throughout and flakes easily with a fork, 15–20 minutes.

To serve, spoon some salsa onto each warmed plate, dividing evenly, and top with the fish medallions.

To prepare: 15 minutes

To cook: 1 hour

4 servings

pork pot roast with parsnips, carrots & apples

1 boneless pork shoulder roast, about 1.5 kg (2¾ lb)

3 Tbsp olive oil

60 g (2 oz) coarsely chopped onion

3 cloves garlic, finely chopped

250 ml (8 fl oz) low-salt chicken stock

3 Tbsp Dijon mustard

2 parsnips, peeled and sliced 2 cm (¾ in) thick

2 carrots, peeled and sliced 2 cm (¾ in) thick

2 firm, sweet apples such as Gala or Golden Delicious, cored and cut into 2 cm (¾ in) pieces

Chopped parsley for garnish

Rub pork roast all over with 1 tsp salt and 1 tsp pepper.

In a flameproof casserole with a lid, heat olive oil over medium-high heat. Add onion and sauté until just translucent, about 3 minutes, add garlic and sauté until garlic is fragrant and golden, about 1 minute more. Using a slotted spoon, remove onion and garlic to a bowl.

Add pork to pot and sear until bottom is browned, about 3 minutes. Using tongs to turn pork, brown all other sides, 3–4 minutes per side. Return garlic and onion to pot and add chicken stock, stirring to scrape up browned bits from bottom of pan. Spread mustard over top of roast and tuck parsnips and carrots around it. Raise heat to high, bring liquid to the boil, then cover and place in oven. Bake for 45 minutes, then remove from oven and add apples, tucking them beneath other vegetables and into juices. Re-cover and cook until a thermometer inserted into centre of meat registers 63°–65°C (145°–150°F) and vegetables and apples are tender, 30 minutes more.

Remove roast to a cutting board and, using a slotted spoon, transfer vegetables and apples to a warmed platter. Cover both loosely with foil and let rest for 10 minutes.

To serve, cut pork into slices about 6 mm (¼ in) thick and arrange overlapping on a warmed platter or on warmed individual plates. Spoon vegetables and apples alongside, sprinkle with parsley and serve.

To prepare: 10 minutes

To cook: 1½ hours, plus 10 minutes to rest

4–6 servings

roasted onions with balsamic & pepper

Peel and quarter several onions. Arrange snugly in a small baking dish, drizzle with olive oil and balsamic vinegar, sprinkle with pepper, and turn to coat. Cover and roast at 180°C (350°F), turning occasionally, until tender, about 1 hour.

roasted mushrooms with sage butter

Mash butter with finely chopped fresh sage, salt and pepper. Arrange mushrooms snugly, stem side up, in a buttered baking dish. Dot with sage butter and scatter with a few sage leaves. Roast in a hot oven until tender and fragrant.

roasted garlic spread with thyme

Cut off top third of 3 garlic heads. Nestle in a baking dish, cut side up and drizzle with olive oil. Roast at 165°C (325°F) until tender, about 1 hour. Squeeze garlic pulp into a bowl and mix in extra-virgin olive oil, cream, thyme, salt and pepper.

pear crumble with lavender

Snugly arrange pear halves, cut side up, in a buttered baking dish. Top with a crumbly mix of cold butter, flour, sugar, and lavender blossoms. Cover and bake until tender, 40 minutes. Uncover and grill until golden. Serve with cream.

roasted fennel
with fennel seed

1 tsp fennel seeds

3 medium fennel bulbs, with stems and fronds still attached, if possible

2 Tbsp olive oil

125 ml (4 fl oz) dry white wine

60 ml (2 fl oz) low-salt vegetable stock, chicken stock or water

Preheat oven to 200°C (400°F). Put fennel seeds in a small sauté pan and toast over low heat, shaking pan frequently so seeds toast evenly, until fragrant, 2–3 minutes. Crush and grind seeds with a mortar and pestle or chop finely using a sharp chef's knife.

Cut stalks from fennel bulbs, reserving a handful of green fronds. If fronds do not look fresh, discard; otherwise, lightly chop enough to measure about 10 g (⅓ oz). Remove any bruised outer leaves from fennel bulbs, then cut bulbs into 4-cm (1½-in) wedges and arrange in a small, shallow baking dish. Drizzle olive oil and wine over fennel and sprinkle with salt to taste and fennel seeds. Add stock and sprinkle chopped fennel fronds over all, if using. Toss to coat evenly.

Cover dish with foil and place in oven. Cook for 30 minutes. Remove foil and continue roasting until fennel is golden, 15–20 minutes more. Fennel should be tender when pierced with a sharp knife. Serve warm.

To prepare: 15 minutes

To cook: 50 minutes

4 side-dish servings

celeriac &
potato gratin

500 g (1 lb) celeriac, peeled and cut into 2.5-cm (1-in) cubes

500 g (1 lb) russet potatoes, peeled and cut into 2.5-cm (1-in) cubes

125 ml (4 fl oz) double cream

60 ml (2 fl oz) semi-skimmed or whole milk

2 Tbsp butter

45 g (1½ oz) grated Parmesan cheese

Preheat oven to 200°C (400°F). Butter a medium baking dish.

In a saucepan, combine celeriac and potatoes with water to cover by 5 cm (2 ins). Add 1 tsp salt and bring to the boil over high heat. Cover and reduce heat to medium. Cook until vegetables are very tender, 10–15 minutes.

Drain vegetables thoroughly in a colander and return to warm saucepan. Add cream, milk, butter and 1 tsp pepper. Using a potato masher or an electric mixer, beat until smooth and creamy.

Spread celeriac mixture evenly in prepared baking dish and sprinkle with Parmesan. Bake until top is lightly browned, 15–20 minutes.

Serve hot, directly from baking dish.

To prepare: 10 minutes

To cook: 35 minutes

6 side-dish servings

spicy cauliflower gratin

1 medium head cauliflower

4 tsp butter

3½ Tbsp plain flour

375 ml (12 fl oz) whole milk

20 g (⅔ oz) fresh breadcrumbs (see Notes, page 117)

1 Tbsp capers, rinsed and drained

1 tsp red pepper flakes

Preheat oven to 200°C (400°F). Butter a medium baking dish.

In a covered steamer over boiling water, cook cauliflower head whole until nearly fork-tender, 15–20 minutes. Remove to a cutting board. When cool enough to handle, cut lengthways into 8 spearlike wedges and arrange in prepared baking dish.

In a saucepan over medium heat, melt 3 tsp butter. When it foams, remove from heat and whisk in flour. Return to medium heat and slowly add milk, whisking constantly. Reduce heat to low, add 1 tsp salt and ½ tsp pepper and cook, whisking occasionally, until taste of flour is gone and sauce is thickened and smooth, about 15 minutes.

Meanwhile, in a small frying pan over medium heat, melt 1 tsp butter. When it foams, add breadcrumbs and cook, stirring often, until golden, 3–4 minutes.

Stir capers and red pepper flakes into white sauce and pour over cauliflower. Sprinkle evenly with toasted crumbs.

Bake until sauce is bubbling and edges are golden, about 30 minutes. Serve hot, directly from baking dish.

To prepare: 10 minutes

To cook: 1 hour

4 servings

parsley mushrooms

4 flat or field mushrooms, brushed clean and stemmed

3 Tbsp olive oil, plus more if needed

6 cloves garlic, coarsely chopped

45 g (1½ oz) fresh parsley leaves, plus sprigs for garnish

Preheat oven to 190°C (375°F). Lightly oil a baking dish just large enough to hold mushrooms in a single layer. Rub caps of mushrooms with 1 Tbsp olive oil.

In a food processor, combine 2 Tbsp olive oil, garlic, parsley leaves, ½ tsp salt and ½ tsp pepper and process until smooth to make *persillade*. If mixture seems too thick, add more olive oil a few drops at a time.

Arrange mushrooms, gill side up, in prepared baking dish. Spread *persillade* on each, dividing evenly and covering gills all the way to the edges. Roast until mushrooms are juicy and tender when pricked with a fork, about 20 minutes. Serve hot, garnished with parsley sprigs.

To prepare: 10 minutes

To cook: 20 minutes

4 side-dish servings

white nectarines
with raw sugar & rum

1 Tbsp butter

4 white nectarines, halved and stoned

8 tsp raw sugar

8 tsp dark rum

Preheat oven to 190°C (375°F). Butter a baking dish just large enough to hold nectarine halves in a single layer. Arrange nectarines, cut side up, in prepared dish.

Put 1 tsp sugar and 1 tsp rum into the cavity of each nectarine half.

Bake until sugar has melted and nectarines are soft but not collapsed, 10–15 minutes. Serve hot or warm.

To prepare: 5 minutes

To cook: 15 minutes

4 dessert servings

baked bananas
& tapioca pudding

90g (3 oz) granulated sugar

3 Tbsp instant tapioca

680 ml (22 fl oz) semi-skimmed or whole milk

1 egg, well beaten

1 tsp vanilla extract

3 barely ripe bananas, still slightly green at the tips

1½ Tbsp lemon juice

1½ Tbsp firmly packed light brown sugar

1 Tbsp butter

Toasted almonds or hazelnuts for garnish (optional; see Note)

In a medium saucepan, combine granulated sugar, tapioca, milk and egg and mix well. Stand for 5 minutes. Place saucepan over medium heat and bring mixture to a full, rolling boil. Remove from heat and stir in vanilla. Cool for 20 minutes, then stir and pour into individual pudding dishes. Refrigerate for up to 12 hours in advance of serving.

Preheat oven to 200°C (400°F). Peel bananas and cut into slices 12 mm (½ in) thick. Butter a shallow baking dish just large enough to hold sliced bananas in a single layer.

Place bananas in a bowl and drizzle with lemon juice, turning several times. Place in prepared baking dish in a crowded or slightly overlapping single layer, sprinkle brown sugar over them and dot with butter. Bake until sugar has melted and formed a syrup, 10–15 minutes.

To serve, spoon warm bananas and some of their syrup on top of tapioca puddings. Garnish with toasted almonds, if desired.

Note: To toast almonds, put in a small, dry frying pan over medium heat. Toast, stirring often, until just starting to turn golden, about 2 minutes; watch carefully or they may burn. Remove at once to a plate. For hazelnuts, spread in a single layer on a baking sheet. Place in oven and toast, stirring occasionally, until golden and fragrant, 10–15 minutes. Pour warm nuts into a clean kitchen towel and rub together to remove skins.

To prepare: 30 minutes

To cook: 30 minutes

5 or 6 servings

swedes   mangoes   pineapples

YELLOW AND ORANGE FRUITS AND VEGETABLES HELP

apricots yellow pears grapefruit

PROMOTE HEART HEALTH • HELP REDUCE THE RISK OF

kumquats   orange   peppers

CERTAIN CANCERS • PROMOTE EYE HEALTH • CONTAIN

carrots pumpkins golden beets

ANTIOXIDANTS FOR HEALING AND PROTECTION • BOOST

yellow apples peaches squash

THE IMMUNE SYSTEM • YELLOW AND ORANGE FRUITS

papayas navel oranges lemons

AND VEGETABLES OFFER ANTIOXIDANTS FOR HEALING

Yellow & orange

The flavours and textures of these bright fruits and vegetables are as vibrant and diverse as their colours suggest. Many members of this yellow and orange group, such as golden beets, potatoes and raspberries, are more commonly found in other colours but the striking hues here signal this group's importance in maintaining a varied menu of health benefits.

In this big family, you'll find an orange fruit or vegetable for every season of the year, from winter's dense, sweet squashes and spring's exotic perfumed mangoes to summer's juicy melon and autumn's starchy sweet potatoes.

In this chapter, the familiar young spring carrot makes an appearance puréed as a bed for roasted sea bass (page 81); squash is baked with butter and honey to echo its natural sweetness (page 87); and golden beets, thinly sliced and roasted, create a backdrop for sea scallops (page 77). Summer's sweet yellow corn, roasted until golden, mixes with fresh crab to fold into a quesadilla (page 77), while winter's pumpkin makes a satiny dessert flan (page 88).

When swede and sweet potatoes are baked with coconut milk and spices, they create a savoury stew perfect for a cold winter night (page 78), while the yellow nectarines of summer, lightly roasted, make a sweet-sour chutney for fish (page 81), and orange peppers and mandarin orange become a sprightly relish for rack of lamb (page 84).

SPRING	SUMMER	AUTUMN	WINTER
carrots	apricots	yellow apples	yellow apples
grapefruit	yellow & orange peppers	dried apricots	dried apricots
golden kiwifruits	corn	golden beets	golden beets
kumquats	mangoes	yellow & orange peppers	carrots
lemons	orange-fleshed melon	lemons	grapefruit
mangoes	nectarines	navel & mandarin oranges	kumquats
navel & mandarin oranges	Valencia oranges	yellow pears	lemons
papayas	papayas	persimmons	navel & mandarin oranges
yellow-fleshed potatoes	peaches	yellow-fleshed potatoes	yellow pears
orange-fleshed winter squash	pineapples	pumpkins	yellow-fleshed potatoes
sweet potatoes	golden raspberries	swedes	pumpkins
	yellow summer squash	orange-fleshed winter squash	swedes
	yellow tomatoes	sweet potatoes	orange-fleshed winter squash
			sweet potatoes

corn & crab quesadillas

½ tsp chilli powder

2 ears yellow corn, husks and silk removed

1½ Tbsp corn or grape seed oil

4 burrito-sized flour tortillas

125 g (4 oz) fresh lump crabmeat, picked over for bits of shell and cartilage

125 g (4 oz) Monterey jack cheese, shredded

10 g (⅓ oz) chopped fresh coriander, plus sprigs for garnish

Preheat oven to 190°C (375°F). In a small bowl, stir together chilli powder, ½ tsp salt and ½ tsp pepper. Rub each ear of corn with 1 tsp oil, then rub with spice mixture. Place in a large baking dish and roast, turning occasionally, until kernels are lightly browned and beginning to wrinkle, about 35 minutes. Remove from oven and set aside until cool enough to handle, then use a heavy knife to cut kernels from cobs.

Divide corn among tortillas, mounding it on one-half of each tortilla. Top corn with equal amounts of crabmeat, cheese and chopped coriander, in that order. Fold filled tortillas in half.

Heat 2½ tsp oil in a large frying pan over medium-high heat. When oil is hot, add filled tortillas and cook until golden on first side, 3–4 minutes. Turn carefully and cook until second side is golden and cheese is melted, 2–3 minutes more. Cook in batches, if needed. Serve hot, whole or cut into wedges, garnished with coriander sprigs.

To prepare: 10 minutes

To cook: 45 minutes

4 servings

scallops with golden beets

4 or 5 golden beets, about 750 g (1½ lb) total, greens trimmed to 5 cm (2 ins)

1 Tbsp plus 2 tsp olive oil

12 sea scallops

2 Tbsp cider vinegar

15 g (½ oz) packed baby rocket leaves

Preheat oven to 180°C (350°F). Rub beets with 1 Tbsp olive oil, ¾ tsp salt and ¾ tsp pepper. Arrange in a baking dish just large enough to hold them in a single layer and roast, turning once or twice, until easily pierced with a sharp knife, about 1¼ hours. Remove from oven and let cool. Trim and peel beets and cut into slices about 6 mm (¼ in) thick. Make a bed of beet slices for scallops on each of 4 plates, dividing evenly.

Pat scallops dry with paper towels and season with salt and pepper. Heat 2 tsp olive oil in a large frying pan over medium-high heat. When oil is hot, swirl pan to coat bottom. Add scallops and sear until golden on first side, about 1½ minutes. Turn and cook until golden on second side and nearly opaque throughout, about 45 seconds more. Add 1 Tbsp cider vinegar and stir to scrape up browned bits from bottom of pan, about 30 seconds. Turn scallops once or twice in the pan juices to give them a light mahogany colour.

Arrange 3 scallops on each bed of beets. Top each portion with a little rocket. Stir 1 Tbsp cider vinegar into pan juices, then drizzle juices over scallops and rocket and serve at once.

To prepare: 10 minutes

To cook: 1 hour 20 minutes

4 servings

baked stew of curried root vegetables

3 Tbsp butter

60 g (2 oz) chopped onion

2 carrots, peeled and cut crossways into rounds 12 mm (½ in) thick

1 parsnip, peeled and cut into 2.5-cm (1-in) cubes

1 large yellow-fleshed sweet potato, peeled and sliced crossways 2.5 cm (1 in) thick, then cut in half

½ head cauliflower, cut into florets

1½ Tbsp plain flour

1½ tsp coriander seeds, crushed

1½ tsp fennel seeds, crushed

1½ tsp ground turmeric

1½ tsp chilli powder

1 tsp ground cumin

60 ml (2 fl oz) low-salt chicken stock

1 tin (430 ml / 14 fl oz) coconut milk

Steamed brown or white rice for serving (optional)

Chopped fresh coriander for garnish

Preheat oven to 200°C (400°F).

In a heavy based frying pan, melt butter over medium-high heat. When it foams, add onion and sauté until translucent, about 2 minutes. Add carrots, parsnip, sweet potato and cauliflower and sauté until vegetables begin to soften, about 10 minutes.

In a small bowl, stir together flour, coriander and fennel seeds, turmeric, chilli powder, cumin, 1 tsp salt and 1 tsp pepper. Sprinkle mixture over vegetables and continue to cook, stirring occasionally, until flour mixture begins to stick to bottom of pot and brown, 3–4 minutes.

Add chicken stock and stir to scrape up browned bits from bottom of pot, then stir in coconut milk. Raise heat to high and bring to the boil, stirring occasionally. Cover, place in oven and bake until vegetables are tender, about 25 minutes.

Remove to a serving bowl and serve hot, spooned over rice, if desired. Garnish with coriander and freshly ground pepper.

To prepare: 20 minutes

To cook: 40 minutes

4–6 servings

halibut with roasted nectarine chutney

Roasted Nectarine Chutney

5 yellow nectarines, halved, stoned, and coarsely chopped

1 Tbsp olive oil

45 g (1½ oz) sultanas

2 Tbsp finely chopped onion

1 tsp lemon juice

1 tsp firmly packed light brown sugar

1 tsp grated fresh ginger

4 halibut steaks, each about 155 g (5 oz) and 2 cm (¾ in) thick

1 Tbsp butter, cut into 4 pieces

For Chutney: Preheat oven to 200°C (400°F). In a small baking dish, combine nectarines, olive oil, sultanas and onion. Turn to coat, then spread evenly in dish. Roast, stirring occasionally, until nectarines are tender, about 15 minutes. Remove from oven. Add lemon juice, brown sugar and ginger and stir to mix well. Taste and adjust seasoning with salt and pepper. Set aside and cover to keep warm.

Lightly oil a baking dish just large enough to hold halibut steaks in a single layer. Season fish on both sides with 1½ tsp salt and 1 tsp pepper, place in prepared dish and top each steak with a piece of butter. Roast until fish is opaque throughout and flakes easily with a fork, 15–20 minutes.

To serve, place a fish steak on each warmed plate and top each with a dollop of chutney. Serve at once and pass remaining chutney at the table.

To prepare: 10 minutes

To cook: 35 minutes

4 servings

roasted sea bass with carrot purée

4 carrots, peeled and cut into 2.5-cm (1-in) pieces

2 Tbsp low-sodium chicken stock

2 Tbsp double cream

3 tsp finely chopped fresh tarragon

4 sea bass steaks, each about 185 g (6 oz) and 2.5 cm (1 in) thick

1 Tbsp butter, cut into 4 pieces

Preheat oven to 200°C (400°F). Butter a baking dish just large enough to hold halibut steaks in a single layer.

In a saucepan, combine carrots with water to cover by 5 cm (2 ins). Add 1 tsp salt and bring to the boil over high heat. Cover and reduce heat to medium. Cook until carrots are tender, 15–20 minutes.

Drain carrots and remove to a blender or food processor. Add chicken stock, cream and 1 tsp tarragon and process to a smooth purée. Taste and adjust seasoning. Spread purée on bottom of prepared baking dish and arrange fish on top. Top each fish steak with a piece of butter and sprinkle with ½ tsp salt and 1 tsp pepper. Roast until fish is opaque throughout and flakes easily with a fork, 15–20 minutes. Place a fish steak and a scoop of purée on each plate and sprinkle with remaining tarragon. Serve at once.

To prepare: 10 minutes

To cook: 40 minutes

4 servings

wild rice with apricots

Sauté cooked wild rice in butter and oil with chopped walnuts, celery and onion until onion is translucent. Mix in chopped dried apricots and season to taste. Scoop into a buttered baking dish, cover and bake in a hot oven for about 30 minutes.

grapefruit baked with brown sugar

Cut grapefruits in half and seed. Using a grapefruit knife, cut around edge of fruit and between sections. Sprinkle each half with 1 Tbsp light brown sugar and bake at 200°C (400°F) until sugar has melted and grapefruit is heated through.

roasted pumpkin purée

Place a small pumpkin on a baking sheet and bake at 180°C (350°F) until flesh pulls away from skin, about 1 hour. Cut pumpkin in half, seed and scoop out flesh. Purée and season with cinnamon, cloves, nutmeg and salt.

baked golden raspberries

Pour a mixture of brandy, brown sugar, honey and vanilla over golden raspberries in a baking dish and dot with butter. Bake, uncovered, at 180°C (350°F) until juices are bubbling, about 20 minutes. Stir gently before serving.

rack of lamb with orange pepper relish

1 rack of lamb, about 875 g (1¾ lb)

1 Tbsp olive oil

1 orange pepper,
seeded and finely chopped

2 Tbsp finely chopped onion

2.5-cm (1-in) piece fresh
ginger, finely chopped

3 Tbsp finely chopped fresh coriander

1 mandarin orange, peeled
and chopped

Preheat oven to 245°C (475°F). Rub lamb all over with 1 tsp salt and 1 tsp pepper. Heat olive oil in a large, non-stick frying pan over medium heat. When hot, add rack of lamb, fat side down and sear until browned, 1–2 minutes. Using tongs to turn and hold the lamb, brown both ends, about 1 minute per end. Finally, sear bone side for 1–2 minutes.

Remove browned rack of lamb to a carving board and cover exposed bones with foil. Place rack, bone side down, in a roasting pan. Roast until a meat thermometer inserted into thickest part of meat (but not touching bone) registers 54°–60°C (130°–140°F) for medium-rare, 13–15 minutes. Transfer to a carving board, tent loosely with foil and rest for 10 minutes.

In a bowl, combine pepper, onion, ginger, coriander, orange and ¼ tsp salt and stir to mix well. Taste and adjust seasoning.

To serve, cut lamb rack into chops. Arrange on a warmed platter and accompany with relish.

To prepare: 10 minutes

To cook: 30 minutes, plus 10 minutes to rest

4 servings

baked sweet potato & swede mash

500 g (1 lb) orange-fleshed sweet potatoes, peeled and cut into slices 2.5 cm (1 in) thick

250 g (8 oz) swede, peeled and cut into slices 2.5 cm (1 in) thick

60 ml (2 fl oz) low-salt chicken stock

1 tsp finely chopped fresh thyme

2 Tbsp butter

2 Tbsp Double cream (optional)

Preheat oven to 180°C (350°F).

In a baking dish, combine sweet potatoes, swede, and chicken stock. Sprinkle with thyme, ½ tsp salt and ½ tsp pepper and turn to mix well. Cover tightly with aluminium foil and bake until vegetables are very tender, about 1¼ hours.

Remove contents of baking dish to a large bowl and add butter. Using a potato masher or electric mixer, mash or beat until fluffy, adding cream, if using. Taste and adjust seasoning. Remove to a warmed serving bowl and serve hot.

To prepare: 10 minutes

To cook: 1¼ hours

4 side-dish servings

spaghetti squash aglio e olio

1 spaghetti squash, about 1 kg (2 lb)

1 Tbsp extra-virgin olive oil

½ tsp finely chopped garlic

30 g (1 oz) finely grated Parmesan cheese

1 tsp finely chopped fresh oregano

Preheat oven to 180°C (350°F). Using a sharp, heavy knife or cleaver, trim stem end from squash, then cut in half lengthways. Scoop out seeds and discard. Place, cut side down, in a baking dish and add 80 ml (3 fl oz) water. Bake until tender, about 1 hour.

Remove squash to a cutting board. When cool enough to handle, use a fork to scrape out flesh in noodlelike strands, scraping all the way to skin. Place squash in a serving bowl, add olive oil, garlic, ½ tsp salt and ½ tsp pepper and stir gently to mix well. Sprinkle with Parmesan and toss to combine. Taste and adjust seasoning. Sprinkle with oregano and serve hot.

To prepare: 10 minutes

To cook: 1 hour, plus 10 minutes to cool

3 or 4 side-dish servings

kabosha squash with honey butter

1 kabosha squash, about 1.25 kg (2½ lb)

2 Tbsp butter

3 Tbsp mild honey such as wildflower or orange blossom

Preheat oven to 190°C (375°F). Place whole squash in a baking dish or on a baking sheet and roast until skin begins to look hard and shiny and pulls away from flesh and squash is easily pieced with a sharp knife, about 2¼ hours.

Just before squash is ready, in a saucepan over medium-high heat, combine butter and honey. Cook, stirring, until butter has melted and honey is incorporated, about 3 minutes. Keep hot.

Remove squash to a cutting board. When cool enough to handle, cut in half and scoop out and discard seeds and coarse strings. Sprinkle flesh with ½ tsp salt and ½ tsp pepper, then scoop it out and spread in a warmed serving dish, breaking up any chunks. Pour honey butter over squash and serve hot.

To prepare: 5 minutes

To cook: 2¼ hours, plus 10 minutes to cool

4 side-dish servings

pumpkin flan

250 g (8 oz) sugar

500 ml (16 fl oz) half-and-half
(half single cream -
half semi-skimmed milk)

250 ml (8 fl oz) whole milk

6 eggs

¼ tsp salt

1 tsp vanilla extract

185 g (6 oz) tinned or homemade
pumpkin purée (page 83)

Preheat oven to 165°C (325°F).

Put 125 g (4 oz) sugar in a 20-cm (8-in) metal pie pan and place on cooker top over medium-low heat. Holding edge of pan with an oven glove, tilt it from side to side until sugar is melted and turns a rich brown colour, about 5 minutes. Remove from heat and set aside.

In a saucepan, combine half-and-half and milk and warm over medium heat until bubbles form around edges, about 5 minutes. At the same time, bring a kettle of water to the boil.

In a bowl, whisk eggs lightly, then add remaining the 125g (4 oz) sugar, salt and vanilla and whisk until sugar dissolves. Slowly pour hot cream mixture into egg mixture, stirring constantly. Stir in pumpkin purée.

Place pie pan with caramel in a roasting pan and pour custard into pie pan. Pour boiling water into roasting pan to come halfway up sides of pie pan. Bake until a knife inserted into middle of flan comes out clean, about 40 minutes.

Remove flan to a wire rack and leave to cool. Serve at room temperature or cover and refrigerate for up to several hours. To unmould flan for serving, slide a knife or spatula around edges. Invert a serving plate over pie pan. Holding pan and serving plate firmly together, flip them, then gently lift off pie pan. Cut into wedges and serve on dessert plates.

To prepare: 20 minutes

To cook: 50 minutes

6 dessert servings

cherries watermelon red plums

RED FRUITS AND VEGETABLES PROVIDE ANTIOXIDANTS

ruby grapefruit radishes beets

FOR PROTECTION AND HEALING • PROMOTE HEART

quinces cranberries raspberries

HEALTH • PROMOTE URINARY TRACT HEALTH • HELP

tomatoes red pears redcurrants

REDUCE THE RISK OF CERTAIN CANCERS • IMPROVE

pomegranates red peppers

MEMORY FUNCTION • RED FRUITS AND VEGETABLES

radicchio strawberries rhubarb

OFFER ANTIOXIDANTS FOR PROTECTION AND HEALING

Red

Red is a colour we especially associate with fruits, from crunchy red apples and juicy red pears to sweet cherries, delicate raspberries, tart pomegranates, mouth-puckering cranberries and gorgeous blood-red oranges and rose-red grapefruit. And even though in the kitchen we treat the tomato, which is rich in lycopene, a powerful red antioxidant, like a vegetable, it is actually one of the wholesome red fruits.

It is tempting to eat fruits out of hand, but cooking them concentrates their sweet flavours. Raspberries shine in a delicate gratin (page 106), while cherries star in a deep-dish cherry pie (page 106). But all these fruits can be used in savoury preparations as well as sweet. When served with rib-eye steak (page 105), roasted red plums echo the savoury flavour of the meat, while tart redcurrants balance rich, oily mackerel (page 99).

The vegetables of the red produce pantry, such as beetroots, radicchio, red potatoes, red onions and radishes, are as versatile as the fruits. Wedges of roasted beetroots, redolent of Indian spices, make an appetising side dish for spring or autumn (page 105). For a hearty weekday main course, roast red potatoes with meaty swordfish fillets (page 99), or, for an easy Sunday supper, put red onions in the pan with the roasting chicken (page 102). Radicchio baked with pasta and blue cheese (page 96) is so satisfying that even a die-hard carnivore won't miss the meat.

SPRING	SUMMER	AUTUMN	WINTER
beetroots	cherries	red apples	red apples
pink or red grapefruit	red peppers	beetroots	beetroots
red onions	red chillis	red peppers	cranberries
blood oranges	red onions	red chillis	pink or red grapefruit
red potatoes	red plums	cranberries	red grapes
radicchio	radishes	red grapes	blood oranges
radishes	raspberries	red pears	pomegranates
rhubarb	strawberries	red plums	red potatoes
strawberries	tomatoes	pomegranates	quinces
redcurrants	watermelon	quinces	radicchio
		red potatoes	radishes
		raspberries	

roasted tomato tart

60 g (2 oz) soft fresh goat's cheese

3 Tbsp semi-skimmed or whole milk

1½ Tbsp finely chopped shallot

1½ tsp fine sea salt

2 Tbsp extra-virgin olive oil

12 plum tomatoes, halved lengthways

1 tsp herbes de Provence

1 partially baked 23-cm (9-in) Tart Shell (below)

Preheat oven to 120°C (250°F). In a bowl, mash cheese with milk, shallot and ½ tsp sea salt to make a spreadable paste. Set aside.

Drizzle about half the olive oil onto a baking sheet and arrange tomatoes on sheet, cut side up. Drizzle with remaining olive oil and sprinkle with herbes de Provence, 1 tsp sea salt and ½ tsp pepper. Roast until tomatoes are soft and have partially collapsed, 1½–2 hours. Remove.

Raise the oven temperature to 190°C (375°F). Spread partially baked tart shell with cheese mixture and top with roasted tomatoes, cut sides up. Return tart to oven and bake until pastry edges are golden, about 15 minutes. Remove and let stand for 15–20 minutes. Cut into wedges and serve warm.

To prepare: 20 minutes

To cook: 2 hours 20 minutes

6–8 servings

tart shell

185 g (6 oz) butter, softened

105 g (3½ oz) caster sugar

2 eggs, lightly beaten

2–3 Tbsp semi-skimmed or whole milk

390 g (12½ oz) plain flour

1 tsp baking powder

90 g (3 oz) cornflour

rape seed oil cooking spray

Cream butter and sugar until fluffy. Beat in eggs and milk to blend. Stir in dry ingredients until mixture comes together in a soft ball. Turn out onto a lightly floured work surface and knead lightly. For a 23 cm (9 in) shell, divide into thirds. For a 25 cm (10 in) shell, divide in half. For tartlets, divide each third into 6 pieces. Press each piece into a disk and wrap in cling film (see Note).

Roll out a dough disk between 2 sheets of cling film to form a round 5 cm (2 ins) larger in diameter than tart pan. Remove film from the top and carefully invert dough into tart pan. With other film still attached, press dough firmly and evenly into pan. Remove film and run rolling pin over top to trim. Chill for 10–15 minutes.

Preheat oven to 165°C (325°F). Cover dough with oiled baking paper or foil. Press evenly into corners of dough and fill with pie weights or dried beans. For a partially baked shell, bake for 15 minutes.
If paper sticks to pastry, bake for a few more minutes; it should come off easily. Remove paper and weights. For a fully baked shell, after removing paper and weights, bake until a pale golden colour, 15–20 minutes more. Leave to cool in pan on a wire rack.

Note: You can refrigerate dough for up to 1 week or freeze for up to 6 months.

To prepare: 30 minutes, plus 10 minutes to chill

To cook: 30 minutes

Three 23-cm (9-in) or two 25-cm (10-in) pastry shells or eighteen 11.5-cm (4½-in) pastry shells

baked pasta with radicchio & blue cheese

375 g (12 oz) rigatoni

1½ Tbsp olive oil

1 head radicchio, cored and coarsely chopped

2 cloves garlic, finely chopped

125 g (4 oz) blue cheese such as Maytag, crumbled

60 ml (2 fl oz) double cream

Preheat oven to 200°C (400°F). Lightly oil a medium flameproof baking dish.

Bring a large pot of salted water to the boil over high heat. Add rigatoni and reduce heat to medium, stirring once or twice. Cook until barely al dente, 12–15 minutes.

Drain thoroughly and place in prepared baking dish. Add ½ Tbsp olive oil and stir to coat evenly.

In a large frying pan, heat 1 Tbsp olive oil over medium-high heat. Add radicchio and garlic and sauté until radicchio wilts and is lightly browned, 7–8 minutes. Stir in 1 tsp salt and pepper to taste, spoon contents of pan into dish with pasta, and mix well.

In a small bowl, mash cheese together with cream until smooth. Add cheese mixture to pasta and radicchio and toss and stir until ingredients are evenly distributed.

Cover with foil and bake until cheese has melted, about 20 minutes. Remove from oven and remove foil.

Preheat grill. Slide dish under grill about 10 cm (4 in) from heat source and grill until top is lightly browned, about 4 minutes. Serve hot, directly from baking dish.

To prepare: 10 minutes

To cook: 50 minutes

4 servings

swordfish with red potato, red pepper & rosemary

375 g (12 oz) medium-sized red potatoes, scrubbed

4 Tbsp olive oil

1 large red pepper, seeded and coarsely chopped

½ red onion, coarsely chopped

2 tsp finely chopped fresh rosemary, plus sprigs for garnish

3 Tbsp dry white wine

500 g (1 lb) swordfish fillets

Preheat oven to 230°C (450°F). Cut potatoes into slices a generous 6 mm (¼ in) thick, then cut slices in half.

In a large, ovenproof frying pan, heat 3 Tbsp olive oil over medium-high heat. Add potatoes, pepper and onion and sprinkle with ½ tsp salt, ½ tsp pepper and remaining 1 tsp finely chopped rosemary. Sauté until potatoes are lightly golden on first side, about 6 minutes. Turn and cook until potatoes are golden on second side and peppers and onions are soft, 6–7 minutes more. Add wine and stir to scrape up browned bits from bottom of pan.

Place fish on top of potatoes and vegetables and sprinkle with ½ tsp salt, ½ tsp pepper and remaining 1 tsp finely chopped rosemary. Drizzle 1 Tbsp olive oil over all. Roast until fish is opaque throughout and flakes easily with a fork, 10–12 minutes. Remove to a platter, garnish with rosemary and serve at once.

To prepare: 15 minutes

To cook: 25 minutes

4 servings

baked mackerel with redcurrants

4 mackerel fillets, about 750 g (1½ lb) total

1 tsp fresh thyme leaves

1 Tbsp plus ½ teaspoon butter

2 Tbsp raspberry vinegar

125 g (4 oz) fresh redcurrants or small grapes

Preheat oven to 200°C (400°F). Butter a baking dish just large enough to hold mackerel fillets in a single layer and arrange fillets in dish. Sprinkle with 1 tsp salt, 1 tsp pepper and thyme. Cut butter into small pieces. Dot fillets with butter and pour vinegar over them. Sprinkle with redcurrants.

Bake until fish is opaque and flakes easily with a fork, 15–20 minutes. Serve hot with pan juices and currants.

To prepare: 10 minutes

To cook: 20 minutes

4 servings

tomatoes stuffed with sausage

Cut off top third of medium tomatoes. Scoop out flesh and pulp and mix with sausagemeat, breadcrumbs, finely chopped onion, beaten egg, parsley, salt and pepper. Stuff tomatoes and bake until sausage is browned, about 40 minutes.

cranberry & blood orange sauce

Bake fresh or frozen cranberries with water and sugar until they begin to soften and are easily mashed, about 20 minutes. Purée with blood orange juice and a little zest. Taste and adjust for sweetness. Serve with meat.

red peppers baked with anchovies

Cut peppers into strips 2.5 cm (1 in) wide. Place in an oiled baking dish, skin side down. Place an anchovy fillet on each, season with salt, pepper and thyme and drizzle with olive oil. Bake in a hot oven until soft, 25 minutes.

roasted beetroot salad with eggs

Rub beetroots with olive oil and roast at 180°C (350°F) until tender, about 1½–2 hours, depending on size. Cut off stems, peel and cut beets into wedges. Toss with vinaigrette, then arrange on lettuce and sprinkle with chopped hard-boiled egg.

poussins with pears

2 poussins

1½ tsp dried lavender blossoms, crushed

1 tsp fresh thyme leaves, plus 2 sprigs

2 Tbsp melted butter, if needed for basting

2 firm but ripe red pears such as red Williams', halved, cored and thinly sliced

3 Tbsp lavender honey

To prepare: 20 minutes

To cook: 1 hour, plus 10 minutes to rest

4 servings

Preheat oven to 180°C (350°F). Pat hens dry inside and out with paper towels, then rub inside and out with lavender, thyme leaves, 2 tsp salt and 1½ tsp pepper. Tuck a thyme sprig into cavity of each hen.

Place hens on a rack in a roasting pan and roast, uncovered, basting once or twice with pan juices or melted butter, until juices run clear when the thigh is pierced with a sharp knife, about 45 minutes.

Remove pan from oven. Add pear slices to pan juices, spreading evenly. Using a pastry brush, glaze hens with 1 Tbsp honey and return to oven. Roast until honey has melted, about 5 minutes. Repeat glazing process twice with remaining honey, roasting for 5 minutes more each time. Remove hens to a cutting board, tent loosely with foil, and rest for 10 minutes. Cover roasting pan with foil to keep pears warm.

To serve, cut each hen in half along backbone with kitchen scissors. Make a bed of pear slices on each warmed plate, dividing evenly, and top each with a half game hen.

Note: You can use wildflower or other honey in place of lavender honey; increase the amount of dried lavender blossoms to 1 Tbsp.

roasted chicken & red onion

1 roasting chicken, 1.5–1.75 g (3–3½ lb)

2 tsp olive oil

2 tsp finely chopped fresh thyme, plus sprigs for garnish

2 large red onions, quartered

1 Tbsp butter, cut into 8 pieces

To prepare: 10 minutes

To cook: 1¼–1½ hours, plus 10 minutes to rest

4 servings

Preheat oven to 180°C (350°F). Rub chicken inside and out with olive oil, then with 1 tsp thyme, 1 tsp salt and ¾ tsp pepper.

Put chicken in a roasting pan and surround with onion quarters. Sprinkle onions with remaining 1 tsp finely chopped thyme, ½ tsp salt and ¼ tsp pepper and top each quarter with a piece of butter.

Roast, basting chicken and onions with pan juices after 30 minutes and then occasionally thereafter, until chicken skin is golden brown and juices run clear when a thigh joint is pierced with a sharp knife, 1¼–1½ hours depending on size of chicken. Remove to a carving board, tent loosely with foil, and rest for 10 minutes.

Carve chicken into serving pieces and arrange on warmed plates with 2 onion quarters alongside each portion. Garnish with thyme sprigs and serve at once.

rib-eye steaks
with baked plums

5 red plums, halved, stoned, and coarsely chopped

2 tsp olive oil

4 rib-eye steaks, about 155 g (5 oz) each

1 Tbsp butter

Preheat oven to 200°C (400°F). Place plums in a baking dish. Coat with olive oil and season with ½ tsp salt.

Put dish in oven and bake until plums are tender and just starting to collapse, 10–15 minutes. Remove to a wire rack and tent loosely with foil to keep warm.

Season steaks generously on both sides with salt and pepper. In a large frying pan, melt butter over medium-high heat. When it foams, add steaks and sear until a deep brown on first side, about 4 minutes. Turn to sear second side and cook to desired doneness, about 4 minutes more for medium-rare.

Remove steaks to warmed plates and spoon warm plums alongside. Serve at once.

To prepare: 10 minutes

To cook: 25 minutes

4 servings

roasted beetroots
with indian spices

1 tsp ground cumin

1 tsp ground coriander

½ tsp ground turmeric

½ tsp ground cloves

6 medium beetroots, stems trimmed to 12 mm (½ in)

2 Tbsp olive oil

Preheat oven to 180°C (350°F). In a small bowl, combine cumin, coriander, turmeric, cloves, 1 tsp salt and 1 tsp pepper and mix well.

Arrange beetroots in a shallow baking dish just large enough to hold them in a single layer. Rub with olive oil, then rub with spice mixture, coating evenly. Roast, turning occasionally, until beetroots are easily pierced with a sharp knife and skins are slightly wrinkled, about 1¼ hours. Leave to cool slightly, then cut off stems and peel.

Cut lengthways into wedges and serve warm or at room temperature.

To prepare: 10 minutes

To cook: 1¼ hours

4 side-dish servings

berry gratin

2 large eggs, separated

3 Tbsp sugar

1 Tbsp crème de cassis

250 g (8 oz) raspberries

250 g (8 oz) strawberries, hulled and halved lengthways

To prepare: 10 minutes

To cook: 15 minutes

4 dessert servings

Preheat grill.

In a bowl, using an electric mixer or a whisk, beat egg whites until soft peaks form when beater or whisk is lifted. Set aside.

In top pan of a double boiler or a heatproof bowl set over (but not touching) simmering water, combine 2 Tbsp sugar and egg yolks and beat with electric mixer or whisk until frothy and thickened, about 10 minutes, scraping down sides of pan or bowl occasionally with a rubber spatula. Remove from heat and stir in crème de cassis. Fold 1 Tbsp of yolk mixture into egg whites, then fold in remaining yolk mixture just until evenly blended.

Divide berries among four 250-ml (8-fl oz) gratin dishes or ramekins and pour egg mixture over them, filling to top. Sprinkle with remaining 1 Tbsp sugar. Place on a baking sheet and slide under grill about 10 cm (4 ins) from heat source. Grill until tops are golden, about 4 minutes. Serve hot or warm.

Note: This dish can also be made as one large gratin.

deep-dish cherry pie

500 g (1 lb) Bing or other sweet red cherries, stoned

200 g (6½ oz) plain flour

250 g (8 oz) sugar

1 tsp baking powder

¼ tsp salt

3 Tbsp cold butter, cut into 12-mm (½-in) cubes

80 ml (3 fl oz) semi-skimmed or whole milk

To prepare: 20 minutes

To cook: 35 minutes

6 dessert servings

Preheat oven to 220°C (425°F). Place cherries in a deep-dish pie dish.

In a bowl, stir together 45 g (1½ oz) flour and sugar. Sprinkle sugar mixture over cherries. In a second bowl, whisk together remaining 155g (5 oz) flour, baking powder and salt. Add butter and cut in with a pastry blender or 2 knives until mixture resembles coarse crumbs. Add milk and stir just until dough holds together, about 30 seconds. Turn out onto a lightly floured work surface and knead several times. Roll out to a 6-mm (¼-in) thickness and lay over cherries; it is not necessary to seal edges or for the cherries to be covered completely.

Bake until crust is golden brown, 15–20 minutes. Reduce oven temperature to 165°C (325°F) and continue baking until cherries are soft and juices are bubbling, 10–15 minutes more. Remove to a wire rack and cool slightly, then serve warm.

soybeans brown rice chick peas

WHOLE GRAINS, LEGUMES, SEEDS AND NUTS PROMOTE

pecans chestnuts bulgur wheat

ARTERY AND HEART HEALTH • HELP REDUCE THE RISK

flaxseed sesame seeds polenta

OF DIABETES • REDUCE HIGH BLOOD PRESSURE • OFFER

pumpkin seeds cashews quinoa

ANTIOXIDANTS FOR PROTECTION AND HEALING • HELP

kasha borlotti beans walnuts

REDUCE THE RISK OF STROKE • MAY REDUCE THE RISK

hazelnuts oats couscous millet

OF CANCERS OF THE BREAST, PROSTATE AND COLON

Brown

Brown is the colour of wholesome, healthy seeds, nuts, legumes and grains. Nuts and seeds are rich in natural oils; legumes deliver a dense, meaty flavour; and grains are typically subtle, making them good vehicles for all kinds of other ingredients and for spices and sauces. All of them, however, are good for you, especially when eaten in their unrefined state.

Legumes are among the most versatile of brown ingredients. Lima beans can be baked with ham to make a hearty main dish (page 123), borlotti beans can be mixed into a duck sausage and tomato casserole reminiscent of classic French cassoulet (page 117), and lentils can be shaped into croquettes and served with brown mushroom gravy (page 113). Dried peas are often used to make soup, but they can also be combined with yoghurt and Indian spices to make a savoury baked purée (page 123).

Grains are ideal in baked goods, such as muffins, but they are also great in filling main dishes, like a robust casserole of pork, quinoa, and chilli (page 120).

Lightly roasting nuts intensifies their flavour for eating out of hand or for enhancing other dishes. Like grains, nuts find their way into desserts, such as a crisp made with pears and cranberries and finished with a walnut topping (page 124), as well as into main courses like a hearty chicken and barley casserole topped with pine nuts (page 114).

GRAINS	LEGUMES	SEEDS	NUTS
amaranth	black beans	dark chocolate	almonds
barley	cannellini beans	coffee beans	Brazil nuts
bulgur wheat	chickpeas	flaxseed	cashews
couscous	kidney beans	pumpkin seeds	chestnuts
kasha (buckwheat groats)	butter beans	sesame seeds	hazelnuts
millet	soybeans	sunflower seeds	macadamia nuts
oats	black-eyed peas		pecans
polenta	split peas		pine nuts
quinoa	lentils		pistachio nuts
brown rice	peanuts		walnuts
whole wheat			

lentil croquettes with mushroom gravy

220 g (7 oz) small green lentils, picked over and rinsed

Gravy

2 Tbsp butter

1 flat or field mushroom, brushed clean, stemmed and chopped

1 Tbsp finely chopped onion

2 Tbsp plain flour

125 ml (4 fl oz) low-salt chicken stock, plus more if needed

About 45 g (1½ oz) fresh breadcrumbs (see page 117)

1 egg

2 Tbsp finely chopped onion

2 Tbsp finely chopped fresh parsley

1 tsp ground cumin

½ tsp ground turmeric

¼ tsp cayenne pepper

2 Tbsp olive oil

In a saucepan over medium-high heat, combine lentils, 625 ml (20 fl oz) water and ¼ tsp salt. Bring to a boil, then reduce heat to low, cover and simmer until lentils are tender, about 20 minutes. (While lentils are cooking, make gravy.) When lentils are tender, drain in a coarse-mesh sieve to remove any excess water.

For Gravy: In a frying pan over medium-high heat, melt butter. When it foams, reduce heat to medium, add mushroom and sauté until it has released some of its juices, 5–6 minutes. Add onion and cook until soft, about 2 minutes. Sprinkle with flour, ½ tsp salt and ¼ tsp pepper and cook, stirring, until flour begins to turn golden, 3–4 minutes. Raise heat to high and add chicken stock a little at a time, stirring with a whisk after each addition. When mixture comes to a boil, reduce heat to low and simmer until flavours meld, 7–8 minutes. If sauce becomes too thick, add a little more stock. Remove from heat and set aside.

Preheat oven to 200°C (400°F). In a bowl, combine lentils, 15 g (½ oz) breadcrumbs, egg, onion, parsley, cumin, turmeric, ½ tsp salt, cayenne and ¼ tsp black pepper. Mix well and shape into 10 patties, each about 12 mm (½ in) thick and 6–7.5 cm (2½–3 ins) in diameter. If mixture is too moist to hold together, add more breadcrumbs. Spread remaining breadcrumbs on a plate or sheet of waxed paper and gently coat each patty in crumbs.

Roast croquettes, until a golden crust forms, about 10 minutes. Turn croquettes and roast until golden brown on second side and crisp, about 5 minutes more.

Reheat gravy to serving temperature. Arrange patties on a warmed platter and serve at once with the gravy.

To prepare: 15 minutes

To cook: 50 minutes

4 servings

chicken, mushroom & barley casserole

105 g (3½ oz) hulled barley

1 Tbsp olive oil

4 skin-on, bone-in chicken thighs

1 Tbsp chopped fresh rosemary

1 stick celery, chopped

2 Tbsp chopped onion

1 clove garlic, finely chopped

30 g (1 oz) pine nuts

250 g (8 oz) brown mushrooms, brushed clean and thinly sliced

60 ml (2 fl oz) low-salt chicken stock

2 spring onions, including tender green parts, chopped

Preheat oven to 200°C (400°F).

Bring a large pot of water to a boil over high heat. Add barley and ½ tsp salt to the pot. Reduce heat to low, cover and simmer until barley is tender and most of water is absorbed, about 45 minutes. Drain in a coarse-mesh sieve to remove any excess water and set aside.

While barley is cooking, in a deep, ovenproof sauté pan, heat olive oil over medium-high heat. When oil is hot, add chicken thighs, skin side down and sprinkle with rosemary, ½ tsp salt and ½ tsp pepper. Cook until first side is golden brown, 4–5 minutes. Turn and cook until second side is golden brown, 4–5 minutes more. Pour off all but 1 Tbsp fat from pan and add celery, onion, garlic and pine nuts. Sauté until vegetables are soft, about 2 minutes.

Stir in barley, mushrooms and chicken stock. Taste and adjust seasoning with salt.

Bake, uncovered, until mushrooms are tender and chicken meat slips easily from bones, 15–20 minutes. During last 5 minutes of baking, sprinkle spring onions over top.

Serve hot, directly from pan or in a warmed serving bowl.

To prepare: 15 minutes

To cook: 1 hour 5 minutes

4 servings

duck sausage, tomato & borlotti bean casserole

2 tsp olive oil

4 duck sausages

3 Tbsp butter

1 onion, thinly sliced

1 tin (375 g/12 oz) chopped tomatoes, with juices

2 tins (470 g/15 oz each) borlotti beans, rinsed and drained

2 tsp finely chopped fresh thyme

1 Tbsp fresh winter savoury leaves or 1 tsp dried

30 g (1 oz) fresh breadcrumbs (see Notes)

To prepare: 10 minutes

To cook: 50 minutes

4–6 servings

Preheat oven to 180°C (350°F). In a frying pan over medium heat, heat olive oil. Add sausages and cook, turning occasionally, until well browned on all sides, 10–12 minutes. Remove to a cutting board and cool.

Melt 1 Tbsp butter in same pan over medium heat, add onion and sauté until onion is very soft and lightly golden, about 15 minutes. Stir in tomatoes and their juices, ½ tsp salt and ½ tsp pepper and cook until tomatoes are heated through, about 5 minutes more. Set aside.

Cut sausage into 2.5-cm (1-in) pieces. In a small saucepan, melt remaining 2 Tbsp butter over medium heat. Set aside.

In a baking dish, combine sausage, beans, thyme, winter savoury, ½ tsp salt and ½ tsp pepper and stir to mix well. Pour tomato mixture over beans and sausage and stir until ingredients are evenly distributed. Top with breadcrumbs and drizzle with melted butter. Bake until topping is golden and juices are bubbling around edges, 15–20 minutes. Serve hot, directly from dish.

Notes: If desired, place the casserole under a grill for 2–3 minutes to brown the top further. To make fresh breadcrumbs, lay country-style bread slices flat on worktop and leave overnight to dry out, or use any type a few days past its peak of freshness. Remove crusts, tear bread into large pieces, and process to crumbs in a blender or food processor. Each bread slice yields 30 g (1 oz) fresh crumbs.

baked potatoes with sesame seed & cheddar

Rub russet potatoes with olive oil and roast at 180°C (350°F) until tender. Slit lengthways about halfway through and spread open. Stuff with shredded Cheddar and sprinkle with sesame seed. Grill just until cheese is melted.

roasted pine nuts & raisin sauce

Roast pine nuts on a baking sheet, stirring occasionally, until lightly golden. Cook raisins in a little water with lemon juice and sugar until raisins are soft and syrup is thickened, about 15 minutes. Stir in pine nuts. Serve with seared tuna.

roasted chestnuts with savoy cabbage

Cut an X through the skin on the flat side of chestnuts and roast at 260°C (500°F) until cut edges curl, 15–20 minutes. Peel and chop. Toss with shredded Savoy cabbage and sauté mixture in butter with thinly sliced onion. Season to taste.

pumpkin seed crust for fish

Finely chop unsalted hulled pumpkin seeds. Brush fish fillets with beaten egg, then roll in chopped seeds. Place on a baking sheet and roast at 180°C (350°F) until fish is opaque throughout, about 20 minutes, depending on thickness.

pork, quinoa
& chilli casserole

2 tsp rape or grape seed oil

90 g (3 oz) quinoa, rinsed
(see Note)

1 Tbsp olive oil

500 g (1 lb) boneless pork loin, cut
into 2.5-cm (1-in) cubes

2–5 green chillis, seeded
and chopped

30 g (1 oz) chopped onion

2 cloves garlic, finely chopped

½–1 tsp chilli powder

½ tsp ground cumin

125 ml (4 fl oz) low-salt chicken stock

30 g (1 oz) shredded Monterey jack
or manchego cheese

12 stoned oil-cured black olives

Preheat oven to 190°C (375°F).

In a saucepan, heat rapeseed oil over medium-high heat. Add quinoa and sauté until grains separate and become opaque, 3–4 minutes. Add 250 ml (8 fl oz) water and ½ tsp salt and bring to the boil. Reduce heat to low, cover and simmer until quinoa is tender, about 12 minutes. Drain in a fine-mesh sieve to remove any excess water and set aside.

In a deep sauté pan, heat olive oil over medium-high heat. When oil is hot, add pork. Sear pork, turning as needed, until lightly browned on all sides, 4–5 minutes. Stir in chillis, onion and garlic, and sprinkle with chilli powder, cumin and ½ tsp salt. Cook until onion is soft, about 2 minutes.

Add chicken stock and stir to scrape up browned bits from bottom of pan. Remove from heat, add quinoa and toss and stir until ingredients are evenly distributed. Remove to a casserole dish if desired. Sprinkle with cheese and dot with olives. Bake, uncovered, until cheese is melted and pork is opaque throughout, about 15 minutes.

Serve hot, directly from baking dish or pot.

Note: Rinse quinoa to remove any soapy-flavoured saponin residue from the seeds. Most of this natural coating is removed by commercial processing, but some can remain. Put the quinoa in a sieve and rinse well as you gently rub the grains between your fingers.

To prepare: 15 minutes

To cook: 40 minutes

4 servings

butter beans
baked with ham

330 g (10½ oz) dried butter beans, picked over and rinsed

500 g (1 lb) ham steak cut into ½ in cubes

1 tsp finely chopped fresh thyme

In a large saucepan over high heat, mix together butter beans, 1 litre (32 fl oz) water and 1 tsp salt and bring to a boil. Reduce heat to low, cover, and simmer until beans are tender, about 1½ hours.

Preheat oven to 200°C (400°F). Cut ham steak into 4 largish pieces.

Ladle beans and their cooking liquid into a medium baking dish. Stir in thyme and ham. Cover with aluminium foil and bake until ham is heated through and has released some of its juices, about 20 minutes.

To serve, ladle beans and stock into warmed bowls, making sure each portion gets an equal amount of ham.

To prepare: 5 minutes

To cook: 2 hours

4 servings

split peas with
yoghurt & mint

220 g (7 oz) green split peas

1 bay leaf

2 tsp extra-virgin olive oil

250 ml (8 fl oz) lowfat or whole plain yoghurt

2 Tbsp chopped fresh mint, plus sprigs for garnish

Rinse peas. In a saucepan over medium-high heat, combine peas and bay leaf with 500 ml (16 fl oz) water, 1½ tsp salt. Bring to the boil, then reduce heat to low and simmer until peas are tender and most of the water is absorbed, about 40 minutes. Drain any excess water.

Preheat oven to 200°C (400°F).

Add ½ tsp pepper to the peas and, using a fork or spoon, mash peas. Taste and season with salt and pepper.

Lightly oil a square, 20-cm (8-in) baking dish and spoon the mashed peas into it, smoothing the top. Drizzle with the remaining olive oil and bake until a light crust forms, about 5 minutes. In a small bowl, stir together yoghurt and chopped mint. Garnish peas with mint sprigs and serve at once with the yoghurt mixture.

To prepare: 10 minutes

To cook: 30 minutes

4 side-dish servings

pear, cranberry & walnut crisp

4 pears, cored and cut lengthways into 6 or 8 slices, depending on size

125 g (4 oz) fresh or frozen cranberries

125 g (4 oz) plain flour

155 g (5 oz) sugar

¼ tsp salt

125 g (4 oz) cold butter, cut into 12-mm (½-in) cubes

60 g (2 oz) chopped walnuts

Preheat oven to 190°C (375°F). Put pears and cranberries in a medium baking dish about 5 cm (2 ins) deep and toss to mix.

Combine flour, sugar and salt in a bowl and whisk to mix well. Using a pastry blender or 2 knives, cut in butter until mixture resembles coarse crumbs. Stir in walnuts. Sprinkle topping evenly over fruit.

Bake until topping is golden brown, fruit is tender and juices are bubbling, 45–50 minutes. Serve hot, warm or at room temperature, directly from baking dish.

To prepare: 15 minutes

To cook: 50 minutes

4–6 dessert servings

oatmeal & dried peach muffins

390 g (12½ oz) plain flour

185 g (6 oz) granulated sugar

2 Tbsp firmly packed light brown sugar

1 Tbsp baking powder

1 tsp cinnamon

½ tsp salt

180 ml (6 fl oz) whole milk

125 ml (4 fl oz) rape or grape seed oil

2 eggs

95g (3 oz) quick-cooking rolled oats

95 g (3 oz) chopped dried peaches

Preheat oven to 180°C (350°F). Grease a muffin pan or line with paper muffin liners.

In a bowl, combine flour, sugars, baking powder, cinnamon and salt and whisk together. In another, larger bowl, combine milk, oil and eggs, whisking together until well blended. Stir flour mixture into milk mixture, stirring just enough to blend all ingredients. Gently stir in oats and peaches.

Spoon batter into prepared muffin cups, filling each about three-quarters full. Bake until muffins are risen and golden brown and a cocktail stick inserted in the middle comes out clean, 25–30 minutes. Let muffins stand for 10 minutes. Turn out onto a wire rack and cool to desired temperature. Serve warm or at room temperature.

To prepare: 20 minutes

To cook: 30 minutes

Makes 18 muffins

Nutrients at work

Humans need more than forty nutrients to support life. Many foods are good sources of these various nutrients, but no single food provides everything. Eating a variety of foods, preferably in their whole form, is the best way to get all the nutrients your body needs. Some nutrients require others for optimal absorption, but excessive amounts may result in health problems.

Until recently, nutritionists believed that the distribution of carbohydrates, protein and fat in a healthy diet to be 55 percent of calories from carbohydrates, 15 percent of calories from protein, and 30 percent of calories from fat. As we have learned more about individual health needs and differences in our metabolism, we have become more flexible in determining what will constitute a well-balanced diet. The table below shows macronutrient ranges recommended in September 2002 by the Institute of Medicine, part of the U.S. National Academies. These ranges are more likely to accommodate everyone's health needs. To help you evaluate and balance your diet as you prepare the recipes in this book, turn to pages 130–33 for nutritional analyses of each recipe.

Nutrition experts have also determined guidelines for vitamins and minerals. For more information, see pages 128–29.

CARBOHYDRATES, PROTEIN, AND FATS

NUTRIENTS AND FOOD SOURCES	FUNCTIONS	RECOMMENDED % OF DAILY CALORIES AND GUIDANCE
Carbohydrates COMPLEX CARBOHYDRATES • Grains, breads, cereals, pastas • Dried beans and peas, lentils • Starchy vegetables (potatoes, corn, green peas)	• Main source of energy for the body • Particularly important for the brain and nervous system • Fibre aids normal digestion	45–65% • Favour complex carbohydrates, especially legumes, vegetables, and whole grains (brown rice; whole-grain bread, pasta and cereal). • Many foods high in complex carbohydrates are also good fibre sources. Among the best are bran cereals, tinned and dried beans, dried fruit, and rolled oats. Recommended daily intake of fibre for adults under age 50 is 25 g for women and 38 g for men. For women over age 50, intake is 21 g; for men, 30 g.
SIMPLE CARBOHYDRATES • Naturally occurring sugars in fruits, vegetables and milk • Added refined sugars in soft drinks, sweets, baked goods, jams and jellies, etc.	• Provide energy	• Fruit and vegetables have naturally occurring sugars but also have vitamins, minerals and phytochemicals. Refined sugar, on the other hand, has little to offer in the way of nutrition, so limit your intake to get the most from your daily calories.

Source: Institute of Medicine. Dietary Reference Intakes for Energy, Carbohydrates, Fibre, Fat, Protein, and Amino Acids (Macronutrients).

CARBOHYDRATES, PROTEIN AND FATS

NUTRIENTS AND FOOD SOURCES	FUNCTIONS	RECOMMENDED % OF DAILY CALORIES AND GUIDANCE
Protein • Foods from animal sources • Dried beans and peas, nuts • Grain products	• Builds and repairs cells • Regulates body processes by providing components for enzymes, hormones, fluid balance, nerve transmission	10–35% • Choose lean sources such as dried beans, fish, poultry, lean cuts of meat, soy and low-fat dairy products most of the time. • Egg yolks are rich in many nutrients but also high in cholesterol; limit to 5 per week.
Fats All fats are mixtures of saturated and unsaturated (polyunsaturated and monounsaturated) types. Polyunsaturated and especially monounsaturated types are more desirable because they promote cardiovascular health.	• Supply essential fatty acids needed for various body processes and to build cell membranes, particularly of the brain and nervous system • Transport certain vitamins	20–35% • Experts disagree about the ideal amount of total fat in the diet. Some say more is fine if it is heart-healthy fat; others recommend limiting total fat. Virtually all experts agree that saturated fat, trans fats, and cholesterol, all of which can raise "bad" (LDL) cholesterol, should be limited.
PRIMARILY SATURATED • Foods from animal sources (meat fat, butter, cheese, cream) • Coconut, palm, palm kernel oils	• Raises blood levels of "bad" (LDL) cholesterol	• Limit saturated fat.
PRIMARILY POLYUNSATURATED (PUFA) • Omega-3 fatty acids: herring, salmon, mackerel, lake trout, sardines, sword-fish, nuts, flaxseed, rapeseed oil, soy-bean oil, tofu • Omega-6: vegetable oils such as corn, soybean, and safflower	• Reduces inflammation; influences blood clotting and blood vessel activity to improve blood flow	• Eat fish at least twice a week. • Substitute PUFA for saturated fat or trans fat when possible.
PRIMARILY MONOUNSATURATED (MUFA) Olive oil, rapeseed oil, sesame oil, avocados, almonds, chicken fat	• Raises blood levels of "good" (HDL) cholesterol	• Substitute MUFA for saturated fat or trans fat when possible.
DIETARY CHOLESTEROL Foods from animal sources (egg yolks, organ meats, cheese, fish roe, meat)	• A structural component of cell membranes and some hormones	• The body makes cholesterol, and some foods contain dietary cholesterol.
TRANS FAT Processed foods, purchased baked goods, margarine and shortening	• Raises blood levels of "bad" (LDL) cholesterol	• Limit trans fat.

VITAMINS

FAT-SOLUBLE VITAMINS AND FOOD SOURCES	FUNCTIONS	DAILY RECOMMENDED INTAKES FOR ADULTS*
Vitamin A Dairy products, deep yellow-orange fruits and vegetables, dark green leafy vegetables, liver, fish, fortified milk, cheese, butter	• Promotes growth and healthy skin and hair • Helps build strong bones and teeth • Works as an antioxidant that may reduce the risk of some cancers and other diseases • Helps night vision • Increases immunity	700 mcg for women 900 mcg for men
Vitamin D Fortified milk, salmon, sardines, herring, butter, liver, fortified cereals, fortified margarine	• Builds bones and teeth • Enhances calcium and phosphorus absorption and regulates blood levels of these nutrients	5–10 mcg
Vitamin E Nuts and seeds, vegetable and seed oils (corn, soybean, sunflower), whole-grain breads and cereals, dark green leafy vegetables, dried beans and peas	• Helps form red blood cells • Improves immunity • Prevents oxidation of "bad" LDL cholesterol • Works as an antioxidant that may reduce the risk of some cancers	15 mg
Vitamin K Dark green leafy vegetables, carrots, asparagus, cauliflower, cabbage, liver, wheat bran, wheat germ, eggs	• Needed for normal blood clotting • Promotes protein synthesis for bone, plasma and organs	90 mcg for women 120 mcg for men

WATER-SOLUBLE VITAMINS

B vitamins Grain products, dried beans and peas, dark green leafy vegetables, dairy products, meat, poultry, fish, eggs, organ meats, milk, brewer's yeast, wheat germ, seeds	• Helps the body use carbohydrates (biotin, B_{12}, niacin, pantothenic acid) • Regulate metabolism of cells and energy production (niacin, pantothenic acid) • Keep the nerves and muscles healthy (thiamin) • Protect against spinal birth defects (folate) • Protect against heart disease (B_6, folate)	• B_6: 1.3–1.5 mg • B_{12}: 2.4 mcg • Biotin: 30 mcg • Niacin: 14 mg niacin equivalents for women; 16 mg for men • Pantothenic acid: 5 mg • Riboflavin: 1.1 mg for women; 1.3 mg for men • Thiamin: 1.1 mg for women; 1.2 mg for men • Folate: 400 mcg
Vitamin C Many fruits and vegetables, especially citrus fruits, broccoli, tomatoes, green peppers, melons, strawberries, potatoes, papayas	• Helps build body tissues • Fights infection and helps heal wounds • Helps body absorb iron and folate • Helps keep gums healthy • Works as an antioxidant	75 mg for women 90 mg for men

Sources: Institute of Medicine reports, 1999–2001

*mcg=micrograms; mg=milligrams

VITAMINS

MINERALS** AND FOOD SOURCES	FUNCTIONS	DAILY RECOMMENDED INTAKES FOR ADULTS*
Calcium Dairy products (especially hard cheese, yoghurt, and milk), fortified juices, sardines and tinned fish eaten with bones, shellfish, tofu (if processed with calcium), dark green leafy vegetables	• Helps build bones and teeth and keep them strong • Helps heart, muscles and nerves work properly	1,000–1,200 mg
Iron Meat, fish, shellfish, egg yolks, dark green leafy vegetables, dried beans and peas, grain products, dried fruits	• Helps red blood cells carry oxygen • Component of enzymes • Strengthens immune system	18 mg for women 8 mg for men
Magnesium Nuts and seeds, whole-grain products, dark green leafy vegetables, dried beans and peas	• Helps build bones and teeth • Helps nerves and muscles work properly • Necessary for DNA and RNA • Necessary for carbohydrate metabolism	310–320 mg for women 400–420 mg for men
Phosphorus Seeds and nuts, meat, poultry, fish, dried beans and peas, dairy products, whole-grain products, eggs, brewer's yeast	• Helps build strong bones and teeth • Has many metabolic functions • Helps body get energy from food	700 mg
Potassium Fruit, vegetables, dried beans and peas, meat, poultry, fish, dairy products, whole grains	• Helps body maintain water and mineral balance • Regulates heartbeat and blood pressure	2,000 mg suggested; no official recommended intake
Selenium Mushrooms, seafood, chicken, organ meats, brown rice, wholemeal bread, peanuts, onions	• Works as an antioxidant with vitamin E to protect cells from damage • Boosts immune function	55 mg
Zinc Oysters, meat, poultry, fish, soybeans, nuts, whole grains, wheat germ	• Helps body metabolise proteins, carbohydrates and alcohol • Helps wounds heal • Needed for growth, immune response and reproduction	8 mg for women 11 mg for men

** The following minerals are generally sufficient in the diet when the minerals listed above are present: chloride, chromium, copper, fluoride, iodine, manganese, molybdenum, sodium, and sulfur. For information on functions and food sources, consult a nutrition book.

Nutritional values

The recipes in this book have been analysed for significant nutrients to help you evaluate your diet and balance your meals throughout the day. Using these calculations, along with the other information in this book, you can create meals that have the optimal balance of nutrients. Having the following nutritional values at your fingertips will help you plan more healthy meals.

Keep in mind that the calculations reflect nutrients per serving unless otherwise noted. Not included in the calculations are optional ingredients or those added to taste, or that are suggested as an alternative or used as a substitution in the recipe, recipe note, or variation. For recipes that yield a range of servings, the calculations are for the middle of that range. Many recipes call for a specific amount of salt and also suggest seasoning food to taste; however, if you are on a low-sodium diet, it is prudent to omit salt. If you have particular concerns about any nutrient needs, consult your doctor.

The numbers for all nutritional values have been rounded using the guidelines required for reporting nutrient levels in the "Nutrition Facts" panel on food labels.

The best way to acquire the nutrients your body needs is through food. However, a balanced multivitamin-mineral supplement or a fortified cereal that does not exceed 100 percent of the daily need for any nutrient is a safe addition to your diet.

WHAT COUNTS AS A SERVING?	HOW MANY SERVINGS DO YOU NEED EACH DAY?		
	For a 1,600-calorie-per-day diet (children 2–6, sedentary women, some older adults)	For a 2,200-calorie-per-day diet (children over 6, teen girls, active women, sedentary men)	For a 2,800-calorie-per-day diet (teen boys, active men)
Fruit Group 1 medium whole fruit such as apple, orange, banana, or pear 60–90 g (2–3 oz) chopped, cooked or tinned fruit 90 g (3 oz) dried fruit 180 ml (6 fl oz) fruit juice	2	3	4
Vegetable Group 30 g (1 oz) raw, leafy vegetables 60–90 g (2–3 oz) other vegetables, cooked or raw 180 ml (6 fl oz) vegetable juice	3	4	5
Bread, Cereal, Rice and Pasta Group 1 slice of bread 180 g (6 oz) ready-to-eat cereal 80 g (2.5 oz) cooked cereal, rice, pasta	6	9	11

Adapted from USDA Dietary Guidelines (2005).

Purple & blue		CALORIES	PROTEIN/ GM	CARBS/ GM	TOT. FAT/ GM	SAT. FAT/ GM	CHOL/ MG	FIBRE/ GM	SODIUM/ MG
p.23	Aubergine crisps with yoghurt dipping sauce	150	5	14	9	2	4	5	208
p.23	Roasted purple carrots & fennel	123	2	16	6	1	0	5	387
p.24	Roasted tuna with olives, grapes & pine nuts	369	35	10	21	3	64	1	924
p.24	Roasted turkey breast with figs & lavender	308	38	17	10	3	95	3	487
p.27	Roasted chicken with purple cabbage	546	47	11	34	10	153	3	784
p.30	Roasted pork & prunes	364	28	29	15	5	82	3	590
p.33	Baked pilaf with currants, lavender & almonds	321	8	52	10	2	8	5	1174
p.33	Roasted blue potatoes with herb tattoos	235	5	39	7	1	0	4	600
p.34	Purple fruits with lavender syrup	194	1	43	3	2	8	1	1
p.34	Roasted black plums with star anise	62	0	12	2	1	5	1	0

Green		CALORIES	PROTEIN/ GM	CARBS/ GM	TOT. FAT/ GM	SAT. FAT/ GM	CHOL/ MG	FIBRE/ GM	SODIUM/ MG
p.41	Roasted sprouting broccoli with lemon	75	2	5	5	1	0	1	308
p.41	Roasted courgettes with anchoiade	256	6	4	24	4	15	1	951
p.42	Spinach soufflé	272	13	11	20	11	252	1	761
p.45	Roasted asparagus with eggs & parmesan	133	9	5	9	2	212	2	237
p.45	Cod on a bed of cucumbers	117	23	3	1	0	54	1	310
p.48	Baked pasta with dandelion greens & sausage	582	31	55	28	8	87	5	1263
p.51	Duck & brussels sprouts	358	22	11	24	3	60	5	88
p.51	Tomatillo casserole	394	43	29	13	2	101	6	1165
p.52	Green apples baked with dried cranberries	264	0	56	6	4	15	3	13
p.52	Green pear & grape clafoutis	254	5	36	10	6	101	1	49

White & tan		CALORIES	PROTEIN/ GM	CARBS/ GM	TOT. FAT/ GM	SAT. FAT/ GM	CHOL/ MG	FIBRE/ GM	SODIUM/ MG
p.59	Baked onion & white aubergine purée	72	2	15	2	0	0	6	586
p.59	Mashed jerusalem artichokes with truffle oil	142	3	21	6	2	10	2	589
p.60	Monkfish with roasted white corn salsa	300	25	17	16	3	40	5	48
p.63	Pork pot roast with parsnips, carrots & apples	425	38	20	22	8	123	4	749
p.66	Roasted fennel with fennel seed	143	2	14	6	7	1	0	92
p.66	Celeriac & potato gratin	210	5	20	13	8	42	3	301
p.69	Spicy cauliflower gratin	161	7	19	7	4	19	4	751
p.69	Parsley mushrooms	134	4	8	11	2	0	2	311
p.70	White nectarines with raw sugar & rum	142	1	22	3	2	8	2	0
p.70	Baked bananas & tapioca pudding	233	5	38	7	4	53	2	59

Yellow & orange		CALORIES	PROTEIN/ GM	CARBS/ GM	TOT. FAT/ GM	SAT. FAT/ GM	CHOL/ MG	FIBRE/ GM	SODIUM/ MG
p.77	Corn & crab quesadillas	360	17	30	19	8	62	2	916
p.77	Scallops with golden beetroots	165	10	18	6	1	14	3	632
p.78	Baked stew of curried root vegetables	270	5	21	20	16	15	6	529
p.81	Halibut with roasted nectarine chutney	327	32	28	10	3	53	4	951
p.81	Roasted sea bass with carrot purée	256	34	8	9	4	92	2	469
p.84	Rack of lamb with orange pepper relish	197	22	6	10	3	81	1	768
p.84	Baked sweet potato & swede mash	132	2	18	6	4	15	4	334
p.87	Spaghetti squash agio e olio	107	3	13	5	1	4	3	857
p.87	Kabosha squash with honey butter	206	3	41	6	4	15	5	302
p.88	Pumpkin flan	343	10	42	16	8	245	1	218

Red		CALORIES	PROTEIN/ GM	CARBS/ GM	TOT. FAT/ GM	SAT. FAT/ GM	CHOL/ MG	FIBRE/ GM	SODIUM/ MG
p.95	Roasted tomato tart	203	4	21	12	5	37	2	489
p.96	Baked pasta with radicchio & blue cheese	520	19	66	21	10	42	3	1001
p.99	Swordfish with red potato, red pepper & rosemary	311	23	18	15	2	83	3	688
p.99	Baked mackerel with currants	436	35	4	30	9	120	1	704
p.102	Poussins with pears	432	29	26	24	7	168	3	1247
p.102	Roasted chicken & red onion	508	45	8	32	9	150	1	717
p.105	Rib-eye steaks with baked plums	254	25	9	13	5	83	1	341
p.105	Roasted beetroots with indian spices	150	3	19	8	1	0	6	732
p.106	Berry gratin	135	4	23	3	1	106	5	36
p.106	Deep-dish cherry pie	319	4	64	6	4	16	2	170

Brown		CALORIES	PROTEIN/ GM	CARBS/ GM	TOT. FAT/ GM	SAT. FAT/ GM	CHOL/ MG	FIBRE/ GM	SODIUM/ MG
p.113	Lentil croquettes with mushroom gravy	334	14	37	15	5	68	8	682
p.114	Chicken, mushroom & barley casserole	325	21	25	16	3	57	5	362
p.117	Duck sausage, tomato & borlotti bean casserole	367	21	30	18	7	55	11	1457
p.120	Pork, quinoa & chilli casserole	365	28	18	20	5	71	2	320
p.123	Butter beans baked with ham	330	35	35	5	2	51	12	2024
p.123	Split peas with yoghurt & mint	218	13	33	4	1	3	16	913
p.124	Pear, cranberry & walnut crisp	401	4	51	22	10	40	5	100
p.124	Oatmeal & dried peach muffins	190	3	28	8	1	25	1	144

Glossary

almonds: The meat found inside the shells of a dry fruit related to peaches, almonds are high in beneficial mono-unsaturated fat and vitamin E, an antioxidant that protects brain cells, promotes heart health, and lowers LDL (bad) cholesterol. They also contain magnesium and omega-3 fatty acids.

anchovies: These tiny Mediterranean fish are high in heart-healthy omega-3 fatty acids. They are generally boned, cured, packed in oil and sold in small tins or jars. White anchovies, known as *boquerones* in Spanish tapas bars and often also packed in vinegar, can be found at speciality-food stores.

apples: The major portion of the apple's nutrition is in its skin, which contains the flavonoid quercetin, an antioxidant that fights viruses and allergies and is thought to be an anticarcinogenic. However, apple flesh is an important source of pectin, a fibre that lowers cholesterol.

apricots: The apricot's colour is due to the pigments beta-carotene and lycopene, which promote eye health and heart health, lower the risk of some cancers and strengthen the immune system. Apricots are also high in vitamin C, potassium and fibre.

asparagus: This vegetable is one of the best sources of folate, a B vitamin that helps fight heart disease. It is also rich in phytochemicals, especially the flavonoid rutin, and a host of vitamins and minerals.

aubergines: The purple skin of the familiar globe aubergine is rich in heart- and brain-healthy anthocyanins, while its flesh contains saponins, antioxidants that help to lower cholesterol levels. Other varieties may be smaller and have lavender, white, rose, green, or variegated skin. The colour of the aubergine's skin does not determine the flavour.

avocados: Technically a fruit, the avocado is high in fat, but most of it is monounsaturated, which helps to lower cholesterol. It also contains beta-sitosterol, a plant cholesterol that lowers cholesterol as well, and may prevent the growth of cancer cells. Avocados are high in vitamins and minerals, especially vitamins A, C, folate, B_6 and potassium.

bananas: Bananas are especially high in potassium, which balances sodium and helps regulate blood pressure and may reduce arterial plaque formation. Potassium also helps to prevent strokes by lowering platelet activity and reducing blood clots. Bananas are also high in vitamins C and B_6 and contain a fibre that may protect against colon cancer.

barley: This grain contributes fibre, vitamins, minerals and phytochemicals to the diet. Hulled barley retains its bran and germ, and so provides more nutrients as well as antioxidants. Pearl barley, which has been refined, steamed and polished, lacks the nutrients of hulled and is not considered a whole grain.

basil: Traditionally used in kitchens throughout the Mediterranean and in Southeast Asia, basil is one of the world's best-loved herbs and is a source of green phytonutrients. Although related to mint, basil tastes faintly of anise and cloves. Italian cooks use it in pesto, often pair it with tomatoes. In Thailand and Vietnam, the local variety of basil (which has more pointed leaves than Italian basil) is often combined with fresh mint for seasoning stir-fries, curries and salads.

beans, borlotti: Usually eaten dried, borlotti beans are cream coloured with many red speckles. High in fibre and protein, they also contain folic acid, iron and potassium.

beans, butter: Also known as lima beans, butter beans are both high in cholesterol-lowering fibre and good source of protein. They contain the minerals molybdenum, which helps your body detoxify sulfites, and magnesium, as well as folic acid.

beetroots: Red beetroots get their colour from the phytochemical betacyanin, which is believed to reduce tumour growth. They also contain betaine, which helps protect the heart, and salicylic acid, which has anti-inflammatory properties, and are especially high in folate. The phytochemicals in golden beets help promote eye health and boost immunity.

blueberries: These native American berries are so high in antioxidant and anti-inflammatory compounds that they are considered "brain food": they contain a range of anthocyanins, which are thought to help fight cancer and have antiageing capabilities. Blueberries are available fresh, dried and frozen.

breadcrumbs: Whether ground from bread a few days past its peak of flavour (fresh crumbs) or bread that has dried completely (dried crumbs), breadcrumbs add texture and body to many recipes. Seek out unseasoned crumbs, which don't contain added salt, dried cheese or other flavourings.

broccoli: Extremely high in vitamin C 60 g (2 oz) provides 68 percent of the daily recommended intake and even higher in vitamin K, broccoli also contains vitamin A and cancer-fighting phytochemicals. Broccoli sprouts also contain high levels of these compounds.

brussels sprouts: These miniature green cabbages contain the same cancer-fighting compounds as their larger cousins, and are even higher in vitamin C and K than broccoli; just 4 Brussels sprouts contain 243 percent of the daily recommended intake of vitamin K, which promotes proper blood clotting.

cabbage: The patriarch of the cruciferous vegetable family, cabbage is high in vitamins C and K, but its real value is its concentration of isothiocyanates, powerful cancer-fighting compounds. Red cabbage contains more vitamin C than green cabbage, along with the antioxidant anthocyanin.

capers: A Mediterranean shrub is the source of these small unopened flower buds. The buds are bitter when raw; once they are dried and packed in brine or salt, they are used to add a pleasantly pungent flavour to a variety of dishes. Capers should be rinsed before use to remove excess brine or salt.

carrots: One carrot provides a whopping 330 percent of the daily recommended intake of vitamin A, which is the source of its fame as a protector of eye health. Carrots are also high in fibre and the bioflavonoids and carotenoids that lower the risk of some cancers, protect the heart and boost immunity. Maroon and purple carrots are colourful alternatives to the common orange carrot, offering different phytochemical benefits, and these colours of carrot are becoming more widely available.

cauliflower: Another member of the large cruciferous family, cauliflower was traditionally blanched, or covered during growing, to keep the head white; now it has been bred to be naturally white. Even so, it still contains the cancer-fighting compounds of its cousins, along with phytochemicals that promote hearth health. Purple cauliflower offers a colourful change of pace from the common white cauliflower.

celery: Like other green vegetables, celery helps to fight certain cancers, promotes eye health, strengthens the immune system and helps build strong bones and teeth. It is also high in fibre.

celeriac: This vegetable is the root of a celery plant grown specifically for its root. Once the knobby brown root is peeled, its tender ivory flesh is delicious. It is lower in carbohydrates than other root vegetables and contains phosphorus and potassium.

cheese, blue: These pungent cheeses are inoculated with the spores of special moulds to develop a fine network of blue veins for a strong, sharp, peppery flavour and a crumbly texture. Most blue cheeses can be crumbled, diced, spread and sliced. Depending on the cheese's moisture content, however, some hold their shape when sliced better than others.

cheese, feta: Young cheese traditionally made from sheep's milk and used in Greek cuisine. It is known for its crumbly texture; some versions are also creamy. Feta's saltiness is heightened by the brine in which the cheese is pickled. Feta is also produced from cow's or goat's milk. Reduced-fat feta is also available.

cherries: Tart bright red and sweet dark red cherries derive their colour from anthocyanin pigments and other antioxidants, which help protect the heart and brain, lower the risk of some cancers and are powerful anti-inflammatories. Cherries also contain a terpenoid that appears to prevent the growth of tumors.

chestnuts: Roasting chestnuts loosens their tough shells and thin, bitter skins. Unlike other nuts, chestnuts do not contain a lot of oil. In addition to carbohydrates, these starchy nuts contain protein, potassium and vitamins B_6 and C.

chicken stock: Many commercial brands are high in salt and may contain MSG, sugar and other ingredients. When shopping, look for tinned stock that is organic or free-range as well as natural, low-salt and fat-free.

chillis: All chillis contain the phytochemical capsaicin, which gives them their hot taste and also acts as a cancer fighter. Although usually eaten only in small amounts, they are nutrient rich, containing vitamins A, C, and E, along with folic acid and potassium.

chives: These slender, bright green stems are used to give an onionlike flavour without the bite. The slender, hollow, grasslike leaves can be snipped with a pair of kitchen scissors to any length and scattered over scrambled eggs, stews, salads, soups, tomatoes or any dish that would benefit from a boost of mild oniony flavour. Chives do not take well to long cooking—they lose flavour and crispness and turn a dull, greyish green.

coriander: This is a distinctly flavoured herb with legions of loyal followers. Used extensively in the cuisines of India, Egypt, Thailand, Vietnam, and China, coriander asserts itself with a flavour that can't be missed. Some describe its taste as being citrusy or minty; others find hints of sage and parsley; some detractors describe it as soapy. It is best used fresh, added at the end of cooking, as it loses flavour after long exposure to heat.

corn: Corn is rich in vitamins, minerals, protein, and fibre. Yellow corn gets its colour from carotenoids that fight heart disease, cancer and ward off macular degeneration.

courgettes: Most of the courgette's nutrients are found in its skin, which contains phytochemicals that strengthen the eyes, bones, and teeth; help to boost immunity; and lower the risk of some cancers.

cranberries: High in both fibre and vitamin C, these red berries are excellent for preventing urinary tract infections due to their polyphenols. The anthocyanins that make cranberries red have antioxidant properties that protect the heart and may guard against cancer. Fresh, frozen and dried cranberries, even juice, are all equally beneficial to health.

crème fraîche: A soured, cultured cream product originating in France, crème fraîche is similar to sour cream. The silken, thick cream, which is 30 percent fat, is tangy and sweet, with a hint of nuttiness. It adds incomparable flavour when used as a topping for berries and pastry desserts. It is also delicious paired with smoked salmon and trout, and lends a velvety smoothness and rich flavour to soups and sauces. Crème fraîche is not always easy to find and many home cooks make their own from heavy (double) cream and buttermilk.

cucumbers: A member of the gourd family, the thinner skin of English cucumbers containing the benificial phytochemicials can be eaten.

currants: Currants are dried grapes. Although smaller than raisins, they have most of the same nutrients.

currants, fresh red: Ripe red currants have a slightly tart taste and are in season at the height of summer (July through early August). They are high in pectin, a natural gelling agent that helps lower cholesterol.

dandelion greens: The sharply saw-toothed leaves of the dandelion have a pleasantly bitter flavour. Like other leafy greens, they contain calcium and iron as well as potassium and vitamins A and C. Be wary of picking the wild greens, which may have been treated with garden chemicals.

fennel: Mild and sweet with an anise like flavour, this pale green bulb contains the phytonutrient anethole, found to reduce inflammation and prevent cancer. Fennel is also a good source of antioxidants, fibre, and vitamin C.

fennel seeds: The seed of the fennel has a liquorice flavour and may be used ground or whole in savoury dishes such as stews and roasts. It is also used in some breads and desserts and to flavour liqueurs.

figs: Whether fresh or dried, figs provide phosphorus, calcium and iron.

fish sauce: Made from a mixture of salted and fermented fish, often anchovies, this salty-tart Southeast Asian sauce adds a depth of flavour to dishes that ordinary salt can't match.

flaxseed: An excellent source of omega-3 fatty acids, these mild, small, reddish brown or deep amber seeds have a crunchy outer shell. They not only help prevent heart disease, but also fight breast and colon cancers and contain calcium, iron, niacin, phosphorus and vitamin E. Refrigerate the seeds and oil to keep them from spoiling.

garlic: Unusually rich in antioxidants and anti-inflammatories, garlic forms organosulfur compounds when chopped, crushed or sliced. These substances lower blood pressure, slow clotting and promote heart health.

ginger: Prized in Chinese cuisine for its culinary and medicinal uses, ginger aids digestion and lowers cholesterol. It contains both antioxidant and antimicrobial compounds.

grapefruit: Half a grapefruit provides 70 percent of the daily recommended intake of vitamin C. Pink or red grapefruits are high in vitamin A as well. Both yellow and pink types contain flavonoids that help guard against cancer, while the latter also has lycopene, a cancer-fighting antioxidant.

grapes: The dark purple Concord grape, which is usually made into grape juice, is extremely high in antioxidants, making grape juice an important heart-healthy food. Red table grapes also promote heart health and immunity, and green grapes can help lower cancer risk and promote eye health.

hazelnuts: Also known as filberts, hazelnuts have sweet, rich cream-coloured flesh. They are a good source of fibre, vitamin E and many minerals including phosphorus, potassium and magnesium.

hominy: Dried corn kernels that have been soaked in an alkali such as lime or lye, washed to remove the outer skin and boiled. This process improves the kernels' flavour makes them more digestible, and helps the body absorb more of their nutrients.

Jerusalem artichokes: Although they are not true artichokes but a kind of sunflower, these tubers have a nutty taste slightly reminiscent of artichokes. They are particularly high in iron and may be eaten either raw or cooked.

kale: A member of the cruciferous vegetable family, kale shares their cancer-fighting abilities. A 90 g (3 oz) serving is high in vitamin A (96 percent of the daily recommended intake), and contains a spectacular amount of vitamin K (590 percent of the daily recommended intake). It has more beta-carotene than broccoli and is an important source of lutein, which promotes eye health.

lavender: You'd have to consume quite a bit of lavender to reap its phytochemical benefits, but it does contain perillyl alcohol, thought to have anti-cancer properties. Lavender's fragrance is also well known for its calming properties.

leeks: By virtue of their membership in the onion family, leeks contain organosulfur compounds, which are thought to fight cancer and heart disease. They also help improve the body's good–bad cholesterol ratio.

lemongrass: A tough, greyish green grass with a bulblike base and mild lemon flavour, lemongrass is a herb of Southeast Asia. It contains a phytochemical, limonene, which is being studied for its anti-tumour properties.

lemons: High in vitamin C, lemons are a flavour enhancer; add lemon juice to raw and cooked fruits and use it to replace salt at the table for vegetables and fish.

lentils: High in protein, like all beans, lentils come in a wide variety of colours. They also provide iron, phosphorus, calcium and vitamins A and B.

lettuces: Lettuce can be divided into four major groups: butterhead, crisphead, leaf, and romaine (cos). Most lettuces are high in vitamins A and C; they also provide calcium and iron. The darker the green, the higher the level of its beneficial phytochemicals, which include the eye-protectant lutein.

limes: High in vitamin C, like all citrus, lime juice also contains lutein, which benefits eye health.

mint: A refreshing herb available in many varieties, with spearmint the most common. Used fresh to flavour a broad range of savoury preparations, including spring lamb, poultry, and vegetables or to decorate desserts.

mushrooms: Neither vegetables or fruits but fungi, mushrooms come in a variety of forms and are available wild and cultivated. They are rich in riboflavin, niacin and pantothenic acid, all B-complex vitamins, and also contain the valuable minerals copper and selenium.

nectarines: A close relative of the peach, the nectarine has an edible skin that contains many of its phytochemicals. Yellow nectarines contain beta-carotene, while the pink-skinned, white-fleshed variety has its own group of beneficial compounds.

nuts: High in fibre, most nuts also contain folate, riboflavin, and magnesium. They are high in beneficial omega-3 fatty acids and vitamin E, an antioxidant that protects brain cells, promotes heart health and lowers LDL (bad) cholesterol.

oats: Oat groats are whole grains that may be cut into pieces to make Scots, or Irish oats, or steamed and rolled into old-fashioned, or rolled, oats. When the groats are cut into pieces and rolled thinner, they become quick-cooking oats. All of these forms retain their selenium and cholesterol-fighting nutrients, unlike instant oats. They are also high in vitamins B_1, B_6, and E.

olives: One of the world's most renowned crops, olives have helped sustain people in the Mediterranean for thousands of years. Too bitter to eat fresh, olives are either pressed to make oil, which is prized for its high levels of vitamin E and heart-healthy monounsaturated fat, or cured.

onions: All onions contain organosulfur compounds that are thought to fight cancer and to promote heart health. Onions also contain quercetin, which boosts these actions, while red onions have the added benefit of the antioxidant anthocyanin.

oranges: Famed for their extremely high vitamin C content, oranges are also high in folate and potassium. They also provide limonoids and flavonoids, two disease-fighting antioxidants. Blood oranges have berry-flavoured red flesh that is high in anthocyanin, an important antioxidant that gives them their dramatic colour.

parsley: With its refreshing, faintly pepper flavour, this vibrant herb is not only widely used, but is also very good for you. It contains cancer-fighting oils, including myristicin, as well as vitamin C, beta-carotene and folic acid.

parsnips: Related to carrots, parsnips are ivory-coloured with a sweet flavour that is enhanced when roasted. They contain vitamin C, folic acid, magnesium and potassium.

peaches: While its fuzzy skin is usually not eaten, the yellow or white flesh of the peach contains the vitamins A and C. Peaches are available fresh, dried and tinned.

pears: The beneficial pigments of pears are concentrated in their skin; as the skin is quite thin (except in the tan-skinned varieties), they can be eaten unpeeled, whether raw or cooked. The flesh contains vitamin A, as well as some phosphorus.

peas: Also called green peas, or garden peas, they should be eaten soon after picking; they are also available frozen. They provide niacin and iron, along with vitamins A and C.

peas, split: When dried, the yellow or green field pea may be split at its natural seam for faster cooking in soups or purées. They are especially high in fibre and contain vitamin A.

peppers: All peppers are high in cancer-fighting phytochemicals; the various compounds that give them their different colours also promote eye health (green, yellow, orange and red); the anti-oxidants in purple peppers aid memory function and promote healthy ageing. Red peppers are high in vitamin C.

Pernod: This anise-flavoured liqueur is popular in France, where it is mixed with water and is served as an aperitif. It is also used in cooking as a flavouring.

pine nuts: Delicate, buttery pine nuts contain both iron and thiamin. They are a favoured garnish for salads and cooked foods.

plums: The edible skin of the plum, which comes in a variety of colours, contains most of its phytochemicals, although the yellow, purple or red flesh also contains beneficial compounds. They are a good source of vitamin C. When they are not in season, enjoy them as prunes, their dried form.

potatoes: The deeper the colour of its pigment, the more healthful phytochemicals a potato possesses, but all potatoes are extremely rich in vitamins and minerals if eaten with the skin; they are also high in fibre. Be sure to buy organic potatoes if you plan to eat the skins.

prunes: These dried prune plums, now also called dried plums, are rich in vitamin A, potassium and fibre. They are higher in antioxidants than any other fruit or vegetable, making them the top antiageing food.

pumpkins: The flesh of the pumpkin is nutrient rich with vitamin A and carotenoids, specifically the cancer-fighters alpha- and beta-carotene and lutein.

pumpkin seeds: High in fibre, protein and various other important minerals, pumpkin seeds also contain beta-sisterol, which lowers cholesterol and slows the growth of abnormal cells. Clean and toast your own, or buy them in natural foods stores.

quinoa: An ancient Incan grain, quinoa is higher in protein than all other grains, and its protein is complete. It is also rich in nutrients and unsaturated fat.

radicchio: A red-leafed member of the chicory family, radicchio has an assertive, bitter flavour, and provides beneficial antioxidants such as anthocyanins and lycopene. Radicchio may be eaten raw, grilled, baked or sautéed.

raisins: Antioxidant rich, raisins are also high in vitamins, minerals and fibre. Both dark raisins and sultanas start as green grapes, but golden raisins are treated to prevent oxidation.

raspberries: Red raspberries have more fibre than most other fruits; they are also high in vitamin C and folate and extremely high in cancer-fighting antioxidants. Golden raspberries are much less common, but they contain heart- and eye-healthy bioflavonoids. Although fresh raspberries are often fragile, frozen unsweetened raspberries retain their flavour and are available year-round.

rice, brown: This whole grain retains its bran covering, making it high in fibre. Brown rice is available in long-, medium-, and short-grain varieties. Like other whole grains, it is high in fibre and selenium; because the bran can become rancid at room temperature, brown rice should be kept refrigerated.

rocket: A peppery green, rocket is eaten both cooked and raw. It is a good source of iron and vitamins A and C and contains lutein, which protects eye health.

rosemary: Used fresh or dried, this Mediterranean herb has a strong, fragrant flavour well suited to meats, poultry, seafood and vegetables. It is a particularly good complement to roasted chicken and lamb.

swedes: This coarse-skinned root vegetable has a mild-tasting orange flesh. It contains vitamins A and C, as well as fibre and potassium.

sesame seeds: Flat and minute, sesame seeds come in several colours, but are most commonly light ivory. They are rich in manganese, copper and calcium, and also contain cholesterol-lowering lignans. Because they have a high oil content, they should be kept refrigerated. Toasting them briefly in a dry frying pan brings out their flavour.

shallots: Another onion family member, the shallot contains the same heart-healthy organosulfides as its relatives. It is milder in taste and more convenient to use in small amounts than the onion.

spaghetti squash: The dense, meaty flesh of winter squashes is rich with vitamins A and C, folate, manganese and potassium, as well as heart-protective and cancer-fighting carotenoids. Bright yellow, oval-shaped spaghetti squash has flesh that forms long, thin strands when cooked. Turban squash has an exotic appearance, and a multihued skin in oranges, yellows and greens.

spinach: High in a multitude of nutrients, from vitamins A, C and K to folate and potassium, spinach is also one of the best sources of lutein, the carotenoid that prevents macular degeneration.

spring onions: Like all onions, spring onions contain organosulfur compounds, which are thought to protect the heart and improve the good/bad cholesterol ratio.

sprouting broccoli: This vegetable, a type of broccoli has a flavour slightly sweeter than broccoli and may be green, white or purple. Like other members of the cabbage family, it is high in vitamins A and C and contains calcium and folate.

squash, summer: Most of the nutrients in summer squash is contained in its bright, edible yellow skin. It is a good source of manganese, as well as the carotenoids that give it its colour.

star anise: A seed-bearing pod from a Chinese evergreen tree, this uniquely shaped spice flavours teas and savoury dishes throughout Asia.

strawberries: Rich in antioxidant content, partly due to their anthocyanin pigments, strawberries are also extremely high in vitamin C. Because of these compounds, as well as their phenolic acids, these berries are thought to be important cancer-fighters.

sugar, raw: Similar in colour and flavour to brown sugar, "raw" sugar is usually refined; however, it may still retain some of the nutrients from the sugarcane plant, which are lost in more refined sugars. Palm sugar, is an unrefined, dark, coarse-grained sugar used in Southeast Asia and India.

sweet potatoes: The most commonly available of these root vegetables are a pale yellow variety and a dark orange one often erroneously referred to as a yam. Both are high in fibre, vitamins A and C, and a host of other vitamins and minerals, as well as more beta-carotene than any other vegetable.

Swiss chard: Another important member of the far-flung cruciferous vegetable family, chard has dark green leaves and either white, yellow or red stalks and ribs. Along with cancer-fighting phytochemicals, it contains iron and vitamins A and C.

tapioca: A starchy substance derived from the root of the cassava plant, tapioca comes in three basic forms, pearl (small dried balls of tapioca starch), granulated (coarsely broken-up pearl tapioca), or quick cooking, also called instant (very finely granulated pearl tapioca).

tomatillos: Sometimes called Mexican green tomatoes, tomatillos are firmer and less juicy than tomatoes and grow to ripeness inside a pale-green papery sheath. Used both raw and cooked, they are an essential sweet-sour ingredient in many Mexican green sauces. Look for fresh or tinned tomatillos in specialist markets.

tomatoes: Not only are tomatoes high in vitamin C, they are also high in fibre and have good amounts of other vitamins and minerals. There are a number of varieties and contain lycopene, which lowers cancer risk. The body absorbs this antioxidant better when tomatoes are cooked, making tomato sauce and tomato paste especially healthful.

vinegar: Made from a variety of red or white wines or, like cider vinegar and rice vinegar, from fruits and grains. Vinegars are seasoned by infusing them with fresh herbs, fruit, garlic or other ingredients. All are a healthy, low-fat way to season a range of foods.

walnuts: Rich, assertive walnuts contain ellagic acid, an important disease and cancer fighter. They are also high in heart-healthy, cholesterol-lowering omega-3 fatty acids and vitamin E. In addition, walnuts protect brain function and contain melatonin, a hormone that aids sleep.

watercress: This spicy green is, surprisingly, a cruciferous vegetable. It contains good amounts of vitamins A and C. The peppery taste of watercress is due to a certain isothio-cyanate that has shown the potential to help combat lung cancer.

wine: The colours of red and rosé wines are due to the skins of the purple grapes used to make the wines; red wine has more beneficial flavonoids than grape juice. These phyto-chemicals have been shown to help increase HDL (good) cholesterol.

winter savoury: This shrublike Mediterranean evergreen herb has a strong, spicy flavour that some cooks liken to thyme. It complements dried beans and lentils, meats, poultry and tomatoes.

yoghurt: The bacterial cultures in yoghurt are prized as a digestive aid. Like the milk it is made from, yoghurt can be full fat, low fat, or fat-free.

Index

BONNIER BOOKS
Appledram Barns, Birdham Road
Chichester, West Sussex PO20 7EQ

Bonnier Books Website
www.bonnierbooks.co.uk

First published in the UK
by Bonnier Books, 2007

WELDON OWEN INC.

Chief Executive Officer John Owen

President and Chief Operating Officer Terry Newell

Chief Financial Officer Christine E. Munson

Vice President International Sales Stuart Laurence

Vice President and Creative Director Gaye Allen

Vice President and Publisher Hannah Rahill

Associate Publisher Sarah Putman Clegg

Associate Editor Lauren Higgins

Art Director and Designer Marisa Kwek

Production Director Chris Hemesath

Colour Manager Teri Bell

Production Manager Todd Rechner

Conceived and produced by Weldon Owen Inc.
814 Montgomery Street, San Francisco, CA 94133
Telephone: 415 291 0100   Fax: 415 291 8841

In collaboration with Williams-Sonoma, Inc.
3250 Van Ness Avenue, San Francisco, CA 94109

A WELDON OWEN PRODUCTION
Copyright © 2007 by Weldon Owen Inc. and Williams-Sonoma Inc.

Set in Vectora

Colour separations by Mission Productions Limited.
Printed and bound in Hong Kong by Midas Printing.

ISBN 13: 978-1-905825-29-5

ACKNOWLEDGEMENTS

Weldon Owen wishes to thank the following people for their generous support in producing this book:
Copy Editor Carrie Bradley; Consulting Editor Sharon Silva; Proofreaders Kate Washington and Lesli Neilson; Indexers Ken DellaPenta,
Heather Belt, Leigh Noe, Jackie Mills; and Ryan Phillips.

Additional photography by Ben Dearnley: page 18 (top left)

Photographer Dan Goldberg

Photographer's Assistant Shawn Convey

Food Stylist Jen Straus

Assistant Food Stylist Max La Rivière-Hedrick

A NOTE ON WEIGHTS AND MEASURES

All recipes include metric and imperial measurements. Metric conversions are based on
a standard developed for these books and have been rounded off. Actual weights may vary.